For the family I had — to Robert, Joan and Sherry in loving memory — and to Will.

For Charlie and the family we have, Daisy and Jack.

Nam Le (Bali Writer's Festival)

"All you get in memoir is lies, what you look for in fiction is truth."

This memoir is not lies but of course it is subjective truth; family events will be remembered differently, varying according to not only our perception at the time but how the event comes to be remembered, and how it is made into a story.

As well as writing plays, an autobiography and articles, my father Robert wrote many letters to his mother and to my mother, Joan. I have quoted from these and, like the books that my mother kept for each of her three children — a mixture of diary, photograph album and scrap book — they have proved an invaluable aid to memory. They have filled the gaps for when I was too young for my memories to be reliable.

Robert at "Fairmans" (1950s)

Robert at the back of "Fairmans" circa 1950

Chapter One

THE QUEEN OF PUDDINGS AND THE PUDDING MAN

I WANTED TO write this book to bring back a lost world. A world lost to me through the deaths of my parents and the sale of the family home, a world swept away. This was the world before supermarkets and pre-packaged, fast or frozen food, before battery chickens or mad cow disease, when milk came in glass bottles with silver or gold foil tops and an inch of cream on the latter, when bananas were exotic and avocadoes unheard of, when a soft drink was Kiora Orange Squash, when salad meant lettuce and Jersey tomatoes with skins as tough as shoe leather and the dressing was Mr Heinz's Salad Cream, when there were cherry orchards a few miles away and the nightingales sang in the bluebell woods. A world in which our address was just four words: "Fairmans Cottage, Wargrave, Berkshire".

After my father died in 1992, I thought going back, going home, would be unbearable. Yet his presence somehow remained, particularly in the Colt House, the little wooden hut by the swimming pool and at the entrance to the woods where he wrote. After he died the Colt

House was gradually abandoned to store mouldering rubber pool toys and his books. But it still smelled of the cigars he only smoked there — my mother didn't like him to smoke in the house. Walking down the gravel path or cutting across the rough grass to the Colt House, I expect him to be there, behind his desk, typing with two fingers on his Olivetti typewriter, the tip of his tongue sticking out as he concentrates or with his feet up on the desk, chair tilted back, reading the *Racing Times*. He always welcomed interruptions so a yell down the length of the garden that he was wanted on the phone or that lunch or tea were in the offing would see him get to his feet and stroll up the path.

In summer he sat at the edge of the pool under the laburnum tree, whose pods one of my small cousins encouraged her baby sister to eat as part of a dollies' tea party, resulting in a dash to hospital. Robert would sit there, straw hat tilted over his face reading one of the thrillers he loved. Round the pool grew small yellow roses which I used to put around the edge of the plate for his birthday cake, as they were always in bloom by the end of May.

"Fairmans"

"Fairmans" was about 40 miles from London and after the M4 motorway was built, you took turning 8/9, emerging at Maidenhead Thicket, which always sounded both romantic and faintly lascivious to me. A little further on, a turn to the left off the main road and you were in the winding Berkshire lanes. The journey would take you past the pub called "The Old House At Home", past the pond and the race-horse stud where baby race horses could be seen frolicking. Then on into the hamlet of Crazies Hill and past Mrs Stacey's thatched cottage, past the school, where my mother used to present the prize for the fancy dress competition and past the entrance to

"The Crazies", an extraordinary mock Palladium building that had once been Henley Town Hall. Then round a narrow dangerous bend where the post office once was and which in my childhood was run by Mr and Mrs Plowman, the oldest looking people I had ever seen.

Finally, down Crazies Hill itself and into the dip in the road which sometimes flooded and where I fell off my tricycle, past the entrance to Penny's Lane which ran along the bottom of our woods and made an interesting if muddy walk. Then another blind corner and you were there, at the back gate of "Fairmans". Walk up the path beside the orchard, past the broken cucumber frames and the ghost of the kitchen garden on your right, the pool in the distance and you came to the back door of the house, which if not open, would at least be unlocked.

When I was a child we all lived in this house, my parents Robert and Joan, the three children, Sherry (Sheridan), five years older than me, me, and Wilton, five years younger. There was also our nanny, Nancy Stubbs. We had a large kitchen garden and grew most of the vegetables we ate. Every kind of food could be bought in the shops in Wargrave High Street, just over a mile from the house. There was a butcher, a fishmonger, a post office, a general store, a greengrocer. In all the shops you placed your order and the shops delivered. The milkman came every day, except Sunday, in an electric cart, and sold bread and cream as well as milk. The farm next door to us sold eggs. People ate a tremendous amount of what today would be considered "unhealthy" food: bacon and eggs and fried bread for breakfast, meat cooked in dripping, lots of butter and full cream milk. There was no such thing as skimmed milk or yoghurt. Vegetables were boiled to mush and fruit was stewed with lots of sugar. No one knew what their cholesterol level was — and yet very few people were overweight. A few people had cars but most people bicycled or walked. Housework required muscle, rugs and carpets were beaten, early vacuum cleaners and floor polishers weighed a ton, washing and mangling was done by hand and lugged to a washing line to be pegged out. Children were turned out of doors to play in all weather and taken for long (boring) walks. As soon as you were old enough, you learned to ride a bicycle.

No strawberry has ever tasted as delicious as those we (or rather the gardeners) grew under nets to protect them from the birds. No new potato or lettuce or pea from the pod ever again had such flavour and sweetness. Roast chicken was a huge treat, we had blackberries, but not blueberries, marrows but not zucchini. We ate seasonally: in spring the first asparagus and new lamb, in summer cherries and raspberries, in late summer damsons and greengages. Autumn was for parsnips, tiny Brussels sprouts, blackberries and crab apples. In winter we looked forward to crumpets for tea and steak and kidney pudding and all the Christmas treats: turkey and Christmas pudding and mince pies with brandy butter.

My grandmother told me that all my mother did before she was married was lie on the sofa and read. This was so uncharacteristic of the mother I knew, who seemed always to be moving. I remember that she always took the upstairs passage (which went down a step, along a bit and then up a step) at a sort of running leap. In my early thirties when I was feeling harassed with small children and a big house, which we were slowly renovating, and no help, and I was in despair over my housekeeping skills (or lack of them), I often thought of my mother and how she organised and ran the house. How everything was clean and orderly (except our bedrooms when we were teenagers), how everything had its place and stayed there or at least was immediately put back there after use. There was a spoon for the jam and a subtly different one for the honey. The days had their appointed tasks, laundry day for instance, and meals had regularity and an order. Never fish on Tuesdays, Friday was the day for fish just as Monday was for cold meat and baked potatoes. Kitchen sinks and kitchen floors and baths and basins were always clean; the airing cupboard had its neat, tidy shelves with all the sheets and towels, pillowcases and tablecloths in their appointed piles. (After my premature and rather precipitous birth at home, I was placed in the airing cupboard because on a freezing June night, it was the warmest place.)

In my mother's kitchen cupboard a whole lot of saucepans and roasting dishes and saucepan lids all sat neatly, not falling out with a terrible clatter as they did from my own kitchen cupboard (and still do.) Of course my mother had help, not my father who never lifted a finger, although he did bring the logs in, but "staff": a cook, "daily" ladies (cleaners), a nanny for us children, two gardeners and a driver for my father.

When Robert acted in London he was driven there and back, the driver doubling as his dresser in the theatre. In the racing season he would also frequently go to the various race courses around England. If he was filming he would be driven to the film studios at Shepperton or Pinewood. The driver also did things like bring down weekend guests, my grandfather or "uncle" Sewell Stokes, Sherry's godfather. The first chauffeur was a chap called Davey who my father poached from the local garage. Davey's head was turned by the bright lights of the West End and while he cooled his heels (my father hadn't yet had the bright idea of Davey combining the roles of driver/theatre dresser) he formed a relationship with a barmaid. Mrs Davey was very cross and partly blamed my father.

John Jonas, also from Gilkes' garage later replaced Davey. He stayed the distance and beyond, watching over my mother when she was widowed and keeping the house ticking over.

Gilkes's garage was at the bottom of the steep hill which led down from where we lived into the village of Wargrave. On the wall as you went down the steepest part was an iron cross; an early car's brakes had failed and the driver had been flung against the wall and killed. Mr Gilkes made a lot of money from the garage business and his son Brian, I remember dark hair in an oiled quiff, married the daughter of a rather grand family, the Hannens.

The queen of puddings

Food was always important in our house, more so to my father than my mother, although she was the one who ordered and bought the food and planned the meals. From Monday to Saturday we had a cook, who came every day about 10.00 am and stayed until 2.30 or so, cooking lunch and often leaving something for supper. The first cook my parents had after the war was called Miss Pleasted. She was large and round and her cooking must have been restrained by post-war rationing. However, her puddings were legendary: treacle tart and treacle sponge, apple snow and apple charlotte, chocolate pudding with pears, queen of puddings and at least once a week pancakes, thin and crisp, golden and mottled, with raspberry jam or sugar and lemon.

Miss Pleasted and the cooks who succeeded her, Mrs Haycock and Mrs Silver, and the "dailies" Mrs Stacey and Mrs George, would stop work every morning for elevenses. They would sit around the kitchen table, the gardeners (Mr Stacey and Mr Smith) would come to the back door and, after meticulously wiping their boots, would stand just inside the door to have their tea. There was only room round that small blue Formica-topped kitchen table for four or, at a squash, five people.

There was tea or cocoa and slices of bread and butter. My treat was to sit with them on Mrs Stacey's comfortable lap or Mrs George's bonier one and be given a little mug of sweet milky cocoa and a slice of bread and butter.

Miss Pleasted cooked on an Aga. This is a solid fuel stove designed by a blind man so it has no sharp edges only rounded corners and no controls except one, a knob you can turn to raised numbers which controls the heat. Grow up cooking on an Aga and no future stove will present much of a challenge. They are, or at least ours was, a tyrannical stove in many ways — fiercely hot or very gently warm with nothing in between. Agas are stunningly good for roasts and meringues, which can be made in the slow bottom oven, often taking five or six hours to cook to a perfect lightly coloured creamy golden crumbliness.

The Aga became later a status symbol for those upwardly mobile Islington and Fulham dwellers who renovated their houses, baked their own bread and forbade their offspring, usually called Prudence, Alice and Harry, television, chocolate and coke. They feature in Joanna Trollope's novels which have been called "Aga Sagas". One such aspiring, trendy London flat dweller installed one in her kitchen only to have it crash through into the flat below.

When Miss Pleasted left us it was to marry the local hedger and ditcher, a slightly sinister figure who lurked in the hedgerows, chopping at things with a small lethal looking sharp instrument, his hat pulled down over his eyes and a cigarette always dangling from his lips. One day my father passed him on the road. Lowering the window Robert enquired after Miss Pleasted. "I suppose she is still a wonderful cook," Robert said wistfully. "I imagine so" replied the ditcher and then with a twist of the knife, "Mind you, I don't let her try anything fancy on me." "Bloody fool" said my father, sotto voce, as he wound up the window.

This version of queen's pudding has a little twist, a layer of plums under the sweetness of custard and meringue

Queen of plums pudding

6 large, firm ripe plums, halved and stoned
275g caster sugar
juice and grated rind of ½ a small lemon
4 eggs
15g butter, softened
125g white breadcrumbs
300ml milk
200ml double cream
½ teaspoon vanilla

Place plums in a medium saucepan with 100g of the sugar, the lemon juice and a little water. Cover and cook gently for 15 minutes then remove the lid and increase the heat. Cook the plums for 10 minutes more until they are very soft; stir them as they cook. Spoon into a well-buttered 2-litre oven proof dish and allow to cool.

Separate 3 of the eggs. Beat 3 yolks with 1 whole egg until smooth. Stir in 25g of the sugar and the lemon zest, butter, breadcrumbs, milk and cream. Leave for 15 minutes to allow the breadcrumbs to swell.

Spoon the bread mixture gently on top of the cooled plums. Spread evenly, bake the pudding for 35-40 minutes in a 160°C fan-forced oven. It should be browned at the edges and only just set. While it is cooking, whisk the egg whites until stiff. Gradually whisk in the remaining 150g of sugar until the meringue is thick and glossy. Beat in the vanilla essence and spoon over the pudding. Replace in the oven and bake at 190°C for about 20 minutes. Serve hot or warm with pouring cream. This is a large pudding which reheats well.

SERVES 6

Instead of treacle tart (which is in fact made with golden syrup) try this tart.

Lime and golden syrup tart

SHORTCRUST PASTRY
- 125g cold butter, cubed
- 250g plain flour
- 1 tbs sugar

FILLING
- 1–1½ cups golden syrup
- 1⅓ cups soft, fresh white breadcrumbs
- 2 tbsp lime juice (lemon juice can be substituted)
- 3 tsp lime zest
- ½ tsp ground ginger
- ½ tsp cardamom

Rub butter into sifted flour until it resembles breadcrumbs, stir in sugar and add enough very cold water to bind dough or buy Careme's vanilla bean short crust pastry. This should be baked blind for about 15–20 minutes.

Heat golden syrup and remove from heat, stir in all other ingredients and pour into the pie crust. Bake at 180°C for about 30 minutes.

You may need more golden syrup and breadcrumbs, I like my treacle tarts not too deep. It is an incredibly rich pudding and vanilla ice cream is a good accompaniment with the warm tart.

SERVES 6

I hope Tate and Lyle never change the design of their golden syrup tins with the dying or wounded lion and the swarm of bees and the motto "Out of the strong came forth sweetness."

We never had sticky date pudding at home; I don't think my parents like dates. Instead, we had something called spotted dick which was a suet pudding with raisins in it. We had the same suet pudding at school but with a jam sauce instead of the raisins and we called it dead man's leg.

Sticky date pudding

> 1¾ cups (300g) dates, coarsely chopped
> 1 tsp bicarbonate of soda
> 1½ cups boiling water
> 90g softened butter
> 1¼ cups (250g) brown sugar
> ½ tsp vanilla
> 3 eggs, beaten lightly
> 1½ cups (225g) self raising flour
> ⅓ cup (40g) pecans
> ⅓ cup walnuts
>
> CARAMEL SAUCE
> 1 cup (200g) firmly packed brown sugar
> 300ml cream
> 100g butter coarsely chopped.

Preheat oven to 180°C. Grease and line the base of a 7cm deep, 22cm (base) cake pan. Place dates and bicarbonate of soda in a bowl. Pour over boiling water. Allow to stand for 20 minutes.

Using an electric mixer, beat butter, sugar and vanilla until pale and creamy. Add eggs, one at a time, beating well after each addition. Using a large metal spoon, fold through date mixture and flour until well combined. Add pecans and walnuts. Spoon mixture into prepared cake pan. Bake for 35 to 40 minutes or until a skewer inserted into the centre comes out clean. Turn onto a plate.

To make the sauce, combine all ingredients in a saucepan over medium heat. Cook, stirring often, until sauce comes to the boil. Reduce heat to medium-low. Simmer for 2 minutes.

Pierce pudding all over with a skewer. Pour ½ cup of warm sauce over warm pudding. Stand for 10 minutes. Cut into wedges. Serve with remaining sauce.

SERVES 4

The pudding man

My father wrote that nothing depressed him more than a meal that didn't finish with pudding. Being taken to restaurants meant sampling the sweet trolley. The first lesson he taught us was: "Never show your hand when being served from a trolley. Never ask for a little of this and a little of that please. If you have decided on profiteroles and syllabub, encourage the waiter to pile your plate with the former, and only when he has put back the spoon, suddenly, and on the spur of the fork, as it were, demand the syllabub." In a *Punch* article he wrote that the two finest puddings he had ever tasted were "…the circular mille feuilles only obtainable at the Chateau de Madrid and an orange Boodle's fool my daughter occasionally makes at the weekends when we have company."

Orange Boodle's fool came from Boodle's Club which was a gentlemen's club, like Buck's (see chapter 5). In an odd synchronicity, Robert's father, my paternal grandfather Wilton Morley, was for a time the club secretary. One summer break he took the petty cash home for safe keeping, gambled it away and had to pawn the canteen of cutlery that had been a wedding present in order to be able to replace the missing money. This was the last straw for my grandmother Daisy. However, this cautionary tale went unheeded: Robert remained a gambler all his life, and the story in no way spoiled his enjoyment of Boodle's fool.

In 1964, a food writer called Arabella Boxer published a revolutionary cookbook. At least the design was revolutionary — it was cut into three horizontal sections: soups and hors d'oeuvre, main dishes, and sweets and savouries. Each recipe was one of four colours: red which denoted richness, a high content of cream, butter, oil or wine; the blue ones were simple dishes with little or no rich ingredients; the grey pages were intermediate; and olive green indicated "Substantial but plain idea like sausages and other filling winter foods". The orange Boodle's fool's page was red.

Orange Boodle's fool
(adapted from *First Slice Your Cookbook* by Arabella Boxer [Thomas Nelson, 1964])

> 4 oranges
> 2 lemons
> sugar to taste
> ⅔ packet of unfilled sponge cakes (450g)
> 600ml thick cream

Cut sponge cakes into squares, about 8cm square, then cut these squares in half horizontally. Grate the rind of two of the oranges and one lemon. Squeeze the juice of all the fruit and strain it. Sweeten to taste (it needs to be quite sharp). Slightly whip the cream and slowly add the juice. Put the sponge cake pieces in a deep soufflé dish and pour over the fruit cream. Refrigerate for several hours.

SERVES 6

The crème de la crème

The eighteenth century food writer Elizabeth Moxon (whose charming book is still in print) would have recommended a posset as medicinal. A posset was sweetened milk or cream to which ale or wine was added and like its cousin, the syllabub, it was given to invalids. Mrs Moxon also includes a recipe for Cowslip Cordial in her book. Whatever happened to cowslips? They were beautiful, yellow flowers, rather like a smaller bluebell, with a distinctive scent, found and picked on childhood walks. They seem to have now disappeared, along with most of the butterflies.

Lemon posset

>   300ml thin cream
>   finely grated zest and juice of 1 lemon
>   ½ cup icing sugar
>   ½ cup sweet dessert wine
>   white of 1 egg
>   finely grated zest of 1 orange

Combine cream and lemon zest in a bowl and whip until the cream is thick. Sift the icing sugar over and pour in the lemon juice and dessert wine. Fold in to combine. In a separate bowl whisk the egg white to soft peaks and fold in. Pour into small glasses or cups, cover with plastic wrap and refrigerate. Top with orange zest before serving.

Serves 4–6

The best pudding made with cream is crème brûlée. The brûlée part can be done under a grill or you can make a caramel and pour it over.

I find the grill less tricky. Watch the little pots like a hawk or they will start curdling round the edges.

Crème brûlée

1 vanilla bean
3 cups (750ml) thickened cream
6 egg yolks
¼ cup (55g) castor sugar and more for the brûlée

Preheat oven to 160°C. Split vanilla bean in half and add to the cream in a saucepan. Heat to just below boiling point. Meanwhile whisk egg yolks and castor sugar in a bowl. Gradually whisk in the hot cream. Place the bowl over a saucepan of hot water and stir for about 10 minutes or until the mixture thickens slightly.

Place six ramekins (½ cup, 125ml) or ovenproof dishes in a baking dish and fill with the custard mixture. Add boiling water to the baking tin, about ¾ of the way up the dishes. Place in the oven for about 20 minutes. Cool, then cover with cling film and refrigerate overnight.

For the brûlée part, place the dishes on an oven tray and heat the grill. Sprinkle the tops with about a teaspoon of castor sugar in an even layer and place under the grill until the sugar melts and colours. You are playing with fire here, literally, but I like the crunchy sugar to be a bit burnt in places.

For an alternative method for the brûlée topping, place 125g granulated sugar and 4 tablespoons of water in a saucepan and bring to the boil without stirring. Allow the caramel to get to a golden brown over high heat, then pour (carefully) over the custards and allow to set. Chill before serving.

Serves 6

Something I make frequently, especially when there is an overabundance of milk is a crème caramel. I always make mine in a very old, heavy, china fluted jelly mould which has room for 500ml of milk and three beaten eggs.

Crème caramel

>500ml milk
>sugar
>vanilla essence
>3 eggs, beaten

Heat the milk with a scant dessertspoon of sugar and a dash of vanilla essence. Meanwhile beat the eggs and then pour the hot milk into them and combine well.

Make a caramel as in the recipe above and pour into the bottom of whatever dish you are using; anything ovenproof will do, a heavy china soufflé dish or a Pyrex dish or even a Pyrex bowl is fine. Bake in a Bain Marie at about 160–180°C. Have a look after 20 minutes or so. If you put a knife blade into the custard you can see if it is set enough. It wants to be wobbly but not runny. When cool, chill in the fridge. Run a knife round the edge of the dish and turn out onto a deep plate. I have taken to covering the top with sliced strawberries. Serve with cream.

If you are nervous about turning it out, just spoon it straight out of the dish it's been cooked in — you will still get that wonderful combination of delicate custard and slightly bitter caramel.

SERVES 4–5

You shall have a fishy on a little dishy

I find fish the most difficult thing to get right. You need a reliable fishmonger who doesn't freeze the left over fish. In Wargrave village the fishmonger was Tony Shaw. He served in the shop in a boater and a striped blue and white apron. He was immensely grand and was always addressed by everyone as Mr Shaw. When my father was offered a knighthood by Harold Wilson he consulted my mother as to whether he should accept it. She advised against it, "Tony Shaw would only charge even more for the fillets of plaice, if I said it was for Lady Morley when I ordered it."

On Fridays we inevitably had fillets of sole or plaice deep fried, with thick chips "hand cut" as a restaurant menu would say these days. My mother always had a grilled Dover sole if we went to a restaurant.

My fish pie

This is a very good tempered dish and you can serve as few as four or as many as eight, just adapt the amounts of fish, prawns, eggs and potatoes.

> 3 salmon steaks or fillets
> 2–3 good sized fillets of firm white fish — orange roughy or red fish or snapper all work well
> 12 large cooked prawns, shelled and roughly chopped
> 3 hard-boiled eggs, quartered
> 4 large potatoes

BÉCHAMEL SAUCE
> milk from cooking the fish plus more milk
> a knob of butter

1–2 tbsp flour
salt and pepper
1 tbs mayonnaise
1 tbs Vermouth or Cinzano
3-4 small pickled cucumbers or gherkins
parsley and/or dill

Gently cook the fish fillets in a large frying pan in a knob of butter and enough milk to cover until it is just cooked and you can flake it off the bone. You want large chunks. Layer the fish in a pie dish, season and add the prawns.

Make a béchamel with the milk the fish has cooked in and stir mayonnaise in at the end. If you like, you can add Vermouth or Cinzano. Pour this over the fish and prawns, add the chopped hard-boiled eggs and gently combine. Add some chopped herbs. Top the pie with potato. You can either mash the potato or slice the potatoes thinly. Par-boil them and then layer on top of the pie and drizzle with melted butter and lots of black pepper.

Even better but a bit more trouble is to boil the potatoes until just tender then, as soon as they are cool enough to handle, grate over the pie on the coarsest bit of the grater. Again, add lots of salt and pepper and drizzle with melted butter. When heated in a hot oven, this topping crisps up and does not have the glug factor of mash potato. Whichever topping you use, serve the pie very hot with green vegetables or a salad.

THIS QUANTITY SERVES 6

My mother always had tins of Portuguese sardines in olive oil in her store cupboard for my father to mash up on brown toast as a late supper or a snack. Sardines are very good for you and if you see fresh ones, preferably fillets, snap them up.

With its combination of currants, pine nuts and orange this is a Sicilian take on sardines.

Stuffed sardines

¼ cup olive oil
70g fresh breadcrumbs
80g pine nuts
75g currants soaked in 1 cup warm water for 20 minutes, drained
2 tbsp finely chopped flat leaf parsley
juice of ½ a lemon and ½ an orange
8 anchovy fillets
18–20 sardines, cleaned and butterflied
12 bay leaves

Heat about a tablespoon of the olive oil in a large frying pan. Add the breadcrumbs and stir continuously over medium heat for about 2 minutes or until they are golden, transfer to a bowl and add pine nuts, currants and parsley. Cool. Add lemon and orange juice and season. Cook the anchovies in a small pan until they are a paste and add them to the mixture.

Place sardines skin side down on a board, place a dessertspoon of stuffing at the wider head end and roll up, starting at the head end, to enclose the stuffing. Place the rolls side by side in a lightly oiled square oven proof dish. Put the bay leaves in between rolls, scatter any remaining stuffing on top and drizzle with olive oil. Season and cook at 180°C for 10–12 minutes, or until sardines are cooked through and crumbs are golden. Serve immediately or at room temperature.

SERVES 6

This is good for a party or as Easter lunch, it will serve 6–8 depending on the appetites of your guests.

Scandinavian baked ocean trout with apple and horseradish sauce

> 2 ocean trout or salmon fillets about 1kg each, pin-boned,
> finely grated rind of 1 lemon
> olive oil
> APPLE AND HORSERADISH SAUCE
> 3 granny smith apples (or bramleys if you can get them) about 500g, peeled and chopped
> 1 tbs horseradish
> 2 tbsp whipped cream

For the sauce combine apples and two tablespoons of water in a saucepan and cook them over medium heat until they have collapsed. Stir until smooth and when cool add horseradish and cream, salt and pepper. Serve at room temperature.

Place one fish fillet, skin side down and sprinkle with grated lemon rind and season to taste, place other fillet on top, skin side up. Rub with olive oil and season, wrap tightly in foil and bake at 200°C for 30 minutes. Let stand, still wrapped, for another 20–30 minutes.

Serve with the apple and horseradish sauce, new potatoes and a watercress salad.

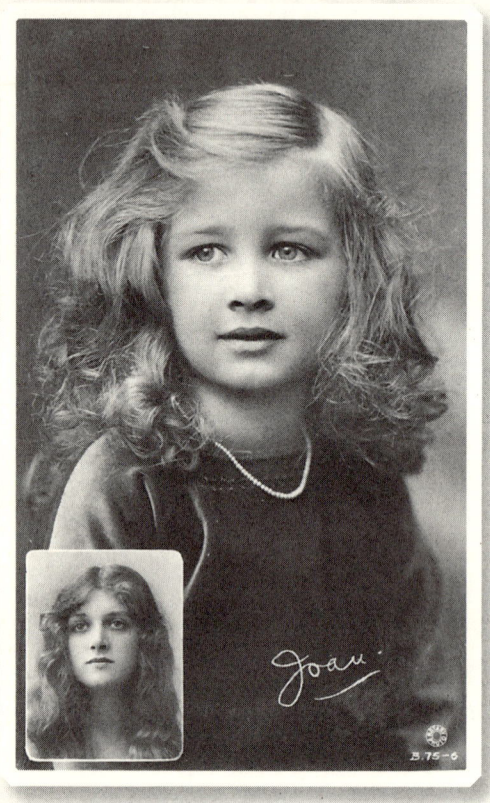

G AND JOAN. JOAN HATED POSING FOR THESE PICTURE POSTCARDS

SALLY, MY MOTHER'S HALF-SISTER.
"A GYPSY VERSION OF GLADYS COOPER"

Robert and Joan on their wedding day
(23rd February 1940, Caxton Hall, London)

Chapter Two

120 WAYS OF USING BREAD

120 Ways of Using Bread has no author, unlike its companion pamphlet, *25 Ways of Using Potatoes* which is by Edith A Browne. They both cost sixpence and Edith's pamphlet went to at least two printings in 1941 and 1942. I found them in a kitchen cupboard when I was clearing out our family home "Fairmans", after my mother died. My parents bought "Fairmans" in 1941, when my mother was pregnant with my older brother, Sheridan, so she had lived there for almost 65 years. A typical Cancerian, she stayed put after my father died in 1992, while the house crumbled gently around her.

In the introduction to *120 Ways of Using Bread*, published by the Millers Mutual Association, is the rather astonishing claim that "… we could live and thrive on bread and milk alone, were it not for the monotony. Every other food we eat — the innumerable comestibles wherewith the shops of grocers, butchers, fruiterers and fishmongers are overflowing — is a luxury. Not a single one of them is an absolute necessity."

On the cover of the pamphlet an attractive dark haired young woman is biting seductively into a small crustless sandwich, while in front of her on the kitchen table is a blue and white striped mixing bowl, empty apart from a wooden spoon, a bottle of milk, two loaves of bread, one white, one brown, three pieces of toast in a toast rack and a plate of crustless sandwiches, garnished by something which looks like a Brussels sprout but must be the heart of a lettuce.

The young woman is astonishingly like my mother in photos from the war years, the same waved dark hair, the same slim figure. There is even the same smile, shy but somehow seductive. Joan hated being photographed because as a child she had had to pose for endless photos with her beautiful mother, the actress Gladys Cooper (always known to me as G). She never forgot an overheard remark to the effect that it was a pity her brother Johnnie had inherited G's beauty and not her. Johnnie was indeed a beautiful blond boy with G's noble profile but Joan had her own remarkable and underplayed beauty. Brought up literally in the theatre by a working mother — G was the manager of the Playhouse Theatre — my mother had an extremely realistic take on the supposed glamour of the theatrical life, on fame and on publicity. When she met my father in 1939, he was just becoming famous and when they married, rather to his chagrin, the newspapers reported: "Gladys Cooper's daughter marries actor."

It was enormously lucky for us, their children, that these two essentially rather shy people met and recognised something in each other. Both were products of failed marriages but each knew they had been loved by both their parents. My father came from a deeply conventional family, at least on *his* mother's side. She was from one of those huge Victorian families, so he had many uncles and aunts. There was an uncle who wore a corset and an aunt who didn't but should have, an uncle who was hopelessly in love with an opera singer and another aunt who took to her bed for decades and then suddenly got up and went around the world.

Robert's father, the Major, was something of a wild card. After his time in the army, he never seemed to have settled to anything: his period of employment at Boodles was one of many more or less failed careers. However, my father had very happy memories of him. His party trick, when a treacle pudding needed the syrup poured over it, was first to stand and then climb onto the dining room table, ending up pouring the syrup from a great height. Once he talked to my father about the facts of life as they walked down Jermyn Street, then a gay cruising zone. "Robbie," he said solemnly, "there are men in this street who paint their faces." My father looked about eagerly, hoping to spot a Red Indian. No further explanation was given.

For many years my father painted his face every night before going on stage. Leichner's 5 and 9 greasepaint, blue eye shadow and then the whole thing powdered over. Since he liked to arrive at the theatre at the last possible moment, Robert was delighted when first pancake makeup and then nothing replaced greasepaint.

So Robert escaped from his somewhat conventional background into the world of the theatre, while my mother exchanged the theatrical world for something that seemed to always completely satisfy her, making a home. We had a conventional middle class upbringing although home revolved around Robert and so was occasionally disrupted by the highs and lows of his chosen career. Whether my parents ever consciously decided that Joan would be the fixed point, the guiding star to Robert's "wandering barque", or whether life just played out that way, it is now too late to ask.

In many ways they were opposites: Joan was tidy, frugal, organised, good with money and responsible; she liked routine, familiar places and people, she was a planner. Robert was untidy, profligate and generous; his attitude to money was "easy come, easy go". "Why wait for the rainy day?" he used to say. "Money is for spending." He liked nothing better than a spontaneous decision, a sudden trip; he could no more see a boat waiting at the end of a jetty but he wanted to be on it and off somewhere. Routine bored him, predictability annoyed him, and responsibility weighed him down. Where these opposites met was in the certainty that "Fairmans" was the home, the heart of the family, the safe haven.

Coming back from a film location or just coming home from the theatre, Robert would throw his hat onto the little chest in the hall, his coat over the banisters, and sink into his arm chair in the sitting room. If there wasn't a meal in the offing he would make himself a sandwich, always brown bread, with pressed tongue (which my mother bought in round glass containers) or he would boil himself an egg. Very occasionally he made himself his version of curry which was cold meat, an onion and some curry powder or corn beef hash: chopped up Fray Bentos corned beef, cooked in a frying pan with an onion and served with a poached egg on top.

Although we might not agree with the bread pamphlet about a diet consisting entirely of bread and milk, there's no denying that bread does play a central role in our cuisine. Recipes from many different countries have ways of using up stale bread, and many have versions of a bread pudding.

English bread and butter pudding, as served up at school lunch, was made with white sliced bread, margarine and a few measly currants or sultanas and custard (probably made with powdered egg). Many versions now will specify brioche or even panettone, but I'm a traditionalist in this respect — white bread and plenty of butter.

Marmalade bread and butter pudding

3–4 slices white bread, crusts removed
30g unsalted butter
2 tbsp marmalade

½ cup sultanas
3 eggs
60g caster sugar
1 teaspoon vanilla extract
250ml milk
250ml cream
2 tsp raw sugar

Butter bread, brush with marmalade, and cut diagonally into quarters. Arrange in two layers in a deep 1.25-litre ovenproof dish. Sprinkle with sultanas. Whisk eggs, sugar, vanilla, milk and cream. Pour liquid over bread and sprinkle with raw sugar. Make sure there is enough liquid to cover bread. Add extra milk if necessary. Set aside for 30 minutes.

Preheat oven to 180°C. Place dish in a large baking tin and fill with enough boiling water to come halfway up sides of dish. Bake for 45–50 minutes, or until custard is set and bread is golden on top.

SERVES 4

The Italian bread salad, Panzanella (below) is a Tuscan recipe; Tuscan bread is typically made without salt and so goes hard and dry very quickly.

Panzanella

8 ripe egg tomatoes, sliced, or the equivalent in mixed "heirloom" tomatoes
½ loaf of a robust Casalinga type bread, cut in slices and dried out a bit in the oven then torn in pieces
2 cloves garlic, crushed
½ bunch basil leaves, chopped
about three small stalks of the centre of a bunch of celery

    20 whole almonds, toasted
    200ml olive oil
    100ml red wine vinegar
    salt and pepper to taste

Combine all the ingredients in one bowl and mix. Dress with olive oil and red wine vinegar. Season with salt and pepper.

Some recipes add 100g grated parmesan but I like it without. I make the salad in advance of serving, adding everything except the almonds and allow the juices to sink into the bread.

SERVES 4–5 AS A STARTER

My parents met just before the outbreak of World War II. My father had spent the summer at Perranporth in Cornwall where his great friend, the actor Peter Bull, ran a repertory company. In 1936 Robert had had a huge personal success playing Oscar Wilde, in a play whose subject matter was considered so scandalous that it had to be performed in the Gate Theatre, Notting Hill which was run as a club theatre. The play transferred to Broadway in 1938–39 and the actor who played Lord Alfred Douglas was Gladys Cooper's son, John Buckmaster. Johnnie and Robert shared a flat and became great friends. Robert was told to look up Johnnie's sister Joan on his return to England. Robert invited Joan and her father Buck to tea and then completely forgot he had issued the invitation. Buck, rather a stickler for conventions, was not best pleased.

A more successful second meeting took place when a mutual friend, Nick Phipps, asked them both to join him at a restaurant and then tactfully didn't turn up.

In October 1939 Robert wrote to Joan: "However awful the war becomes I shall always remember that at the beginning of it I met you and was happy because of you."

In November he wrote to her: "I think there is only one place I shall ever be really happy ever again and that isn't America or England or anywhere except very deep in your arms."

They married in February 1940 and lived initially in a block of flats that had an anti-aircraft gun on the roof. When the sirens went off and the gun fired, all the standard lamps in the flat fell over. Robert used to say that this made him very nervous but that Joan had nerves of steel. By the following year they were looking for somewhere out of London. Robert needed to be close to the film studios at Denham, Buckinghamshire where he filmed throughout the war. Given a low medical rating because of his flat feet and the fact that he was virtually blind in one eye, he nevertheless lived with a certain amount of trepidation that he might be called up in some capacity or other, so he took care to remain in work, filming and then acting in touring plays.

My parents found "Fairmans" through an advertisement in *The Times*. The cottage was in the Thames Valley, about a mile and a half from Wargrave station on the Great Western train line out of Paddington Station. Wargrave had started out with the more romantic name of Weirgrove but ended up with this rather gloomier corruption. A local builder had bought a derelict cottage on the local estate, Hennerton, as a project for his men to work on when business in the building trade was slow, reasoning that if the men were working they wouldn't be called up.

The cottage had no name but was marked simply as "cottage" on the map my father was shown by the builder-owner. The woods at the back of the cottage were marked as "Fairman's" so reading down the map, my father thought the cottage was called "Fairman's Cottage" and that is what it became.

It consisted then of two rooms up, and two rooms down, a kitchen and a bathroom. No electricity and no mains drainage. The builder was laying the last of the terracotta flagstones on the ground floor when my parents arrived. He named a price and Robert offered him a slightly lower one; the builder stood up and shook Robert's hand. They'd bought a house.

Until they made a garden, the house was surrounded by trees like a house in a fairy story. My father thought he should buy the woods at the back of the house so he asked the owner, a Mr Slyfield, if he was willing to sell. Mr Slyfield explained that the woods were no use to *him*, as he put it he'd "had the oak out of them." This was to build the Nissan huts for the airmen on the airfield at Crazies Hill, a mile and a half from "Fairmans".

The house was added onto twice. A bigger bathroom and a bedroom upstairs and downstairs plus a nursery were added during the war. Then, in 1948, while we went off round the world a sitting room and a bedroom, dressing room and bathroom were added onto the other end of the house. During this time my aunt Margaret and her daughters, Catherine and Felicity lived in the house.

The family tree

At my first school, Rupert House in Henley, we were given sheets of paper and told to draw a family tree. When I asked the teacher for a second sheet a few minutes later she asked me if I had made a mistake. I said I hadn't, that I need a larger piece of paper; in fact I was putting the pieces side by side. This was because both my mother's parents had been married three times and I wanted to include all the half and step children this involved. By Buck, my grandfather, G had my mother and my uncle John, then G married Neville Pearson and they had Sally, my mother's much younger half-sister. (Neville Pearson had been married before to an eccentric society beauty called Mary Mond who once appeared, as her guests assembled for a party, stark naked except for a rope of pearls which reached her pubic hair. They had a son, Nigel.) My grandmother's third husband, Philip Merivale, had four more or less grown up children by his first wife. Two boys and two girls. Daniel, who farmed in Africa and was accidently killed when he tripped while carrying a loaded shotgun, and John, who was always known as Jack, an actor. The girls were Valentine, who married a school master, had two children and died tragically young of breast cancer, and Rosamond who was my mother's contemporary and great friend, also an actress.

Buck had no more children; his second wife, Nellie Taylor, a beautiful actress, died of tuberculosis. He then married Grace Barford, the daughter of Lord Ashley. She had three Barford children; Caroline and Clive who were twins and Edwina, who became my godmother.

Of the Merivales, Jack was most in evidence at "Barn Elms", my grandmother's Henley house. I sensed he had a rather ambivalent attitude towards G. He knew his father had been in thrall to her and he felt she hadn't always treated Philip very well. Jack was rather cynical and could be very sharp. After Laurence Olivier left Vivien Leigh and married Joan Plowright, Jack became Vivien's lover and protector. He seemed to be able to deal with her manic depressive episodes rather better than Larry had been able to, but perhaps it was simply that there were not so many of them and maybe by that time there was better treatment available. She died of a recurrence of tuberculosis, while Jack, who had been acting and had come home from the theatre, was making himself some soup.

Jack then had a long liaison with, and finally married, the delightful actress Dinah Sheridan. The family always felt that it was poetic justice that Jack, who had cared beautifully for Vivien should, when he fell ill with kidney disease, be lovingly looked after by Dinah.

Jack brought Vivien to tea at "Fairmans" once and we sat out on the lawn; there was not much trace of the extraordinary beauty. I was expecting to meet Scarlett O'Hara of course or Lady Hamilton and not a distinctly middle aged woman, rather formally dressed for a summer tea on a lawn. Before they went back to London my father suggested a drink and Vivien said she would have a glass of white wine. This threw my parents into some consternation; my father had to admit there was gin and whisky and sherry but no wine. Didn't my parents have a cellar, she enquired? Will, aged about ten, piped up that we had a cupboard under the stairs where we kept the coca cola.

My aunt Rosamond was rather unhappily married to a Canadian. She eventually left Canada with her two little daughters and came to live near my grandmother in Oxfordshire. With very little money my aunt Rosamond still managed to remain one of the most beautiful and stylish women, as well as being one of the gentlest and kindest. Ros continued to act a bit and was in the last play my grandmother did, a revival of *The Chalk Garden*.

My closest relatives Sally and Johnnie were both alarming in their different ways.

Johnnie was a schizophrenic who resided occasionally at "Barn Elms" and sometimes stayed with us. He spent the latter part of his life in mental hospitals, first in Northampton and later in the Priory, a well-known, if not notorious clinic, in Richmond. He possessed many and various talents as a young man: actor, a cabaret performer, writer and painter, as well as being a man of astonishing beauty. It was therefore a family tragedy that he was overtaken by what was then a more or less untreatable disease. A crisis came when he had a violent psychotic episode in New York in 1952 and was put in Bellevue the hospital for the criminally insane.

G was playing in London in Noel Coward's *Relative Values*. Noel was one of the people instrumental in getting Johnnie released from Bellevue and the charges against him dropped, on condition he leave the USA. G wrote to thank Noel for all he had done: "I am torn with anxiety and heartbreak by the knowledge of the unhappiness of my beloved John, but the Countess in your play is as merry as a grig eight times a week… laugh, clown, laugh."

With the progression of his illness and the attendant skewing of his thought processes Johnnie came to blame his parents for his illness and refused to see them. My mother Joan was the only family member he would see.

My aunt Sally was terrifying to Will and me as small children because she was very sharp with us. Amazingly beautiful, she was accurately described as being like a gypsy version of Gladys Cooper. After several tempestuous love affairs she finally fell in love with the actor Robert Hardy, always known as Tim, and they bought a beautiful house at Upper Bolney, a few miles beyond Henley. Here they brought up two daughters in a ménage which included a donkey, ponies, horses, dogs and peacocks. I envied Emma and Justine for the wonderfully ramshackle rather bohemian existence they seemed to have and they in their turn envied us for the order and tranquillity of "Fairmans", regular meals, a nanny and no raised voices which were sometimes a feature of life at Upper Bolney. Sally and Tim eventually decided to divorce and Sally upped sticks and moved to London where she still lives in a flat up many flights of stairs. Emma is a renowned photographer and Justine a writer and great India-phile, who devotes herself to healing the damaged psyches of the Kashmiris.

Although my grandfather Buck had four brothers and sisters, we didn't know anything about any of them. He had been more or less disowned by his family when he married G, who herself was briefly disowned by her father for eloping with Buck. Thus their children were never allowed to meet the more respectable cousins. Buck's father was a clergyman, so it must have come as a shock when his son began to make his living as a bookie and then married an actress. When Johnnie, G and Buck's son was born Buck said, "I was determined he should never be afraid to tell me everything. When I got into trouble, which was often, I only had one thought and that was to keep it from my father, I hoped it would be the other way about with John." (From *Buck's Book* (Grayson and Grayson, 1933) p. 126.)

G's two sisters, though, were very much presences in the family.

Gracie, G's youngest sister was born deaf. Although her forward-thinking parents had her educated at a special school, she always needed to live within the family circle, first with her mother and later on with G. After G died she came to live with my parents. She and G had a fairly stormy relationship. She was rather bullied by G into doing many of the more menial housekeeping tasks like washing up. In fact, my grandmother, extolling the virtues of an early dishwasher to my mother, explained: "It's simply wonderful, you just put all the dirty cups and plates in and then, when it's time for tea, Gracie takes them out and washes them up."

Gracie would frequently ignore G when she was trying to get Gracie's attention (probably to tell her to do something) and then, in exasperation, G would throw a cushion at her. Gracie was tiny and birdlike, pretty rather than beautiful, although she had been stunning as a young woman. Gracie was very proud of her hands and like G had incredibly long, strong fingernails always painted blood red. She was very bright, her intuition making up for her deafness, a sophisticated observer and a very good mimic. She could lip read, use sign language and speak, albeit in the atonal way of the profoundly deaf. She was full of life.

The middle Cooper sister was Doris. She had also tried to be an actress but her first appearance on stage was in a play in which G was the star. She played a maid and her confidence was sapped when she thought the audience was hissing at her. A fellow cast member had to reassure her that it was simply many people all whispering to their neighbour: "That's Doris Cooper, she's Gladys Cooper's sister."

Doris took up with an actor much given to serial matrimony, adopted his late wife's child (she had committed suicide) and had a daughter of her own; she brought up both the girls when he went off to America. As well as working as a housekeeper she was helped financially by my grandmother, my father and Ivor Novello who was particularly fond of her. Life was hard for her and I'm sure with some justification she thought my grandmother had had an easy life in comparison. They quarrelled often and G never forgave Doris for having the last word when my grandmother made some comment about "that terrible little man you married" and Doris's riposte was: "Darlin, I never married him!"

I came to know Doris well when she was getting on in years and we were living near her in London. She used to come and have supper with us at least once a week and even babysat for us. Like my grandmother she had an indomitable spirit with no self-pity and, like my grandmother, she adored her daughters and their children.

If there is anything more comforting for a family meal than a roast chicken, I have yet to discover it. One thing that enhances a roast chook is stuffing, but it's boring to stop and fiddle around when you want to get the dinner in the oven so here is my invention: two-minute stuffing for chicken.

Two-minute roast chicken stuffing

a couple of slices of white bread, torn up
1 onion
parsley, sage, thyme or whatever is to hand
100g cold butter

In a food processor, put bread and roughly chopped onion and herbs. Blitz to process. Add cold butter, chopped. Blitz again.

Finely grated lemon rind is a nice addition. Season well and stuff the chicken with this, no pre-cooking.

Roast chicken with pumpkin and black lentils

(adapted from a Diana Henry recipe that featured in the UK *Telegraph*)

1 roast chicken
1kg pumpkin
6 tbsp olive oil
sherry to baste
225g black lentils
½ onion
1 stalk of celery
1 bay leaf
thyme (to taste)
1 tbs lemon juice

Roast chicken in the usual way, surrounded by pumpkin, peeled and cut into wedges. Chicken and pumpkin should have 3–4 tablespoons of olive oil over them. At the end of roasting baste chicken with a couple of tablespoons of sherry.

While the chicken is roasting cook lentils in a saucepan, covered with water and add chopped onion and celery, bay leaf and some thyme. Cook about 25–30 minutes until tender but not mushy. Drain and add 2 tablespoons olive oil and then lemon juice.

Carve the chicken, surround with pumpkins and lentils and scatter with the picada.

PICADA — SPANISH THICKENING FOR A SAUCE

40g hazelnuts (not blanched)
100ml olive oil
30g chewy peasant-style bread, sliced about 1cm thick
zest from ½ orange, finely chopped
1 clove garlic
2 tbsp finely chopped flat-leaf parsley
1 tbs sherry vinegar

Toast hazelnuts and rub in a tea towel to remove the skins, chop coarsely. Fry the bread in olive oil and when cool, blitz in a food processor with all the other ingredients.

On Robert's side of the family there was his only sister, my Aunt Margaret and her two daughters, Catherine and Felicity. Margaret lived in Kent. Margaret and Robert were chalk and cheese and although deeply fond of each other they could only be in each other's company for a few minutes without some argument ensuing. When Margaret came to stay for a weekend, you could estimate the time before there would be raised voices and my mother would have to step in with some diversionary tactic.

Like many siblings, Robert and Margaret knew exactly which buttons to push to elicit an instant response. Although they adored each other they could go from genuine delight at being in each other's company back to the rivalry and teasing of the nursery in about ten minutes.

THE FAMILY IN NEW YORK, WINTER 1948-49

Sherry and Abbie (Sydney, 1949)

My christening, Autumn 1946

First passport photos

Chapter Three

COMING INTO THE WORLD AND GOING ROUND IT

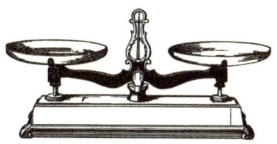

Western Union Telegram: pm June 10 1946 to Merivale, 750 Napoli Drive, Pacific Palisades, California:
"Your granddaughter arrived here rather unexpectedly this morning stop Both well stop Buck here too for quiet weekend love from us all to you all Joan."

My BIRTH went down in family folklore. I arrived six weeks early on a cold Bank Holiday Monday morning. The District Nurse just beat me to it; the doctor didn't arrive until after the event. My mother apologised to the District Nurse that all was not in apple pie order. The District Nurse explained that she had just come from the gipsy encampment up on Crazies Hill common where she had been delivering a baby in the top bunk of the caravan whilst the old grandfather lay dying in the bottom bunk. So this, she told my mother, is heaven.

My grandfather Buck, done out of his quiet weekend, amused himself by standing by the gate and warning passing motorists that the dip in the road at the bottom of Crazies Hill had flooded and cars would be unlikely to be able get through the water. He refused to allow my father to be indoors while my mother was in labour so they perambulated round the garden in the pre-dawn chill. "I'm sure Joannie wouldn't mind if we went indoors," said Robert pathetically, but Buck was a stickler for form. After all the excitement and my safe arrival, Buck and Robert were asked to put up the cot. When they proved obviously incapable of doing this, my mother got out of bed and did it herself. As I was very small, an estimated weight of 4lbs (2 kilos) and my leg was the length and width of Robert's forefinger, it was considered a good idea to put me in the airing cupboard.

When my father came into the bedroom he found that the nurse had laid me on the bed where I was being gently licked my mother's Pekineses. When he queried how hygienic this was, she told him firmly it would get me used to germs.

The time came to give me a name. Robert always said *Annabel* was on the first page of the book of babies' names and I was lucky I wasn't named *Ankaret* which came immediately above it. My second name Evelyn was to honour Robert's favourite aunt. As soon as I could talk I became Abbie, my own version of Annabel.

My baby book is pink leather with *Baby's Book* on the front. As she did for both Sherry and Will, my mother kept a meticulous record of what happened in our lives, often written in the first person. So I know, for instance, that April 7 1948 was the first time I travelled by train and that I "was very good." Because this first book records as far as Christmas 1948 it includes the arrival of Nancy Stubbs who came to be our nanny in January 1948. She came with us to America in the summer of that year when Robert took *Edward My Son*, the play he had co-written, first for a season on Broadway and later to Sydney and Melbourne, after a successful run in the West End (see chapter 12).

Sherry as a baby had been looked after by Old Nan who had been my mother's nanny. In a letter from G to Buck in early 1916, she notes: "Joan is in her bath in an awful temper. She has just told Nannie she is worse than the Germans!"

Old Nan was tiny and dumpy. There is a picture of her holding me, aged one month. She wears a white blouse, a darker skirt and a little black cap perched on the top of her head, tied with wide ribbons under the chin, rather in the style of Queen Victoria. When she retired she lived in a cottage in Wargrave village with her sister Alice. It was there that I pushed my beloved bear on wheels, Brumas, under the kitchen table before we went to America and from where I retrieved him three years later. In the meantime Old Nan had died.

When my father flew back to England briefly in 1949, he wrote to my mother:

"I went down to see Alice this evening…(she) told me about Nan and how well the Nurse and Doctor had looked after her. When Alice asked her whether she would like you (Joan) or John to come over she said 'Oh dear no, it would only upset them. I like to think they are with their Mummie.' Rather, as Alice said, as if she was handing back her charges. I liked too the story of her asking Alice to ask the Doctor not to sit on her next time he came and when Alice said that she didn't think it was very likely he would, she assured her he had on his last visit, adding: 'I think he's good, but he's getting very old!'"

America

When Old Nan retired, Nancy Stubbs, who didn't wear a uniform as some nannies did at the time, became our nanny. She came with us to America.

First stop was G's house in Napoli Drive, Pacific Palisades. The Californian house with its wide verandas overlooked a golf course and had a swimming pool which was where Sherry and I spent most of our time. The first time I went in the pool I announced I was "flabbergasted", and when I fell in on a later occasion and was fished out I said proudly: "Abbie dived".

G was filming *The Secret Garden* at MGM studios. I was taken on the set and met the animals and birds used in the film; a raven, silver foxes, lambs and squirrels. Greta Garbo who was quite a pal of G's came to lunch and *we* went to lunch at George Cukor's. There were lots of picnic teas on the beach at Malibu. G had a beach lot there and I apparently spent my time running in and out of the sea.

I loved dressing up and being read *Alice In Wonderland*. I had an imaginary friend called Nigel and a favourite doll, Mary Anne. Jamie Niven gave me a black doll as a birthday present. Apparently I came downstairs and announced "Mary Anne has had a baby in the night" and produced the black doll. Jamie and his brother David were David Niven's sons and had recently acquired a stepmother. Their mother Primmie, David's first wife, had tragically fallen down a flight of cellar stairs playing a game of sardines at a Hollywood party. My mother thought the Niven boys the best behaved children in Hollywood. My portrait was painted by an artist called Eileen Chandler, in a favourite pale blue party dress with ruffles, smocking and a sash. I had a birthday party to which Liza Minnelli and Charlie Chaplin's son, Michael, came.

In November we went to New York, to a large apartment on Park Avenue. There was snow by late December and, as Sherry got a sleigh for Christmas, we went sleigh riding in Central Park.

From Robert's letters to his mother:

"Sherry had a party on Valentine's Day, we had about 20 children all rather wilder than they are at home but I must say rather nice in a curious uninhibited way. Four of them fell on the model railway but otherwise there was no damage done. We showed them a couple of

films on Gladys' projector. Ivor Novello is here on his way to Jamaica and I took him and Zena Dare, Adrianne Allen and one or two others to hear Gracie Fields who is singing in cabaret. She was as wonderful as ever. A film actress called Jean Arthur is coming to tea as we are supposed to be doing a broadcast. She doesn't know if her voice will sound funny next to mine. Of course it will but I don't see that it matters. Had supper last night with some people called the Loders, he's the brother of Basil Loder who used to be on the stage and her first husband was a multi-millionaire. I had quite a long chat with Mrs Randolph Hearst who agreed with me it didn't pay to leave children money. Hearst has five sons, I believe, all millionaires and all quite horrible. Freddie Lonsdale was at the party, who I liked enormously. Also Rex (Harrison) and Lili (Palmer) and Cedric Hardwicke, a bit disgruntled.

Adrienne gave a farewell party for Ivor. Joannie and I were rather dreading it as there was going to be a lot of singing by Olive Gilbert. However we escaped comparatively unscathed with only two songs. Mrs Syrie Maugham, Somerset Maugham's wife was there and I liked her every much. She is a great friend of Gladys. Cyril Richards and his wife and Zena Dare made the affair just like home, except for Greta Garbo."

My mother added a post script: "I always though English children's parties were exhausting but they're nothing compared to having American children — they're so rowdy! We kept them quiet for a bit showing films."

After New York we went back to California, had a holiday in Hawaii with G and then it was on to Australia.

In California G had a rotisserie in her oven, a spit on which she roasted the most delicious legs of lamb; I love roast lamb and we eat it at least once a week. Here's a recipe with a Middle Eastern flavour.

Spring roast lamb with mint yoghurt sauce
(adapted from *Gourmet Traveller*, October 2010)

    120g blanched almonds
    2 tsp cumin
    1 tsp coriander seeds, dry roasted and ground
    8 dates, pitted and finely chopped
    olive oil
    ½ lemon thinly sliced and chopped
    2 cups firmly packed mint, chopped
    ¾ cup flat leaf parsley, chopped
    3 cloves garlic, crushed
    1 tsp paprika
    large pinch cinnamon
    olive oil
    1 boneless lamb shoulder
    6 carrots, sliced lengthwise

MINT YOGHURT SAUCE
    1 cup loosely packed mint, chopped
    400g thick natural yoghurt
    juice of ½ a lemon

Roast almonds at 180°C for 5–7 minutes then roughly chop.

Mix almonds, spices, dates and herbs with a good slug of olive oil. Spread on opened lamb shoulder. Roll and tie with string. Place carrots on base of oiled baking tin with lamb on top. Drizzle with olive oil and roast at 180°C for 1½–1¾ hours or until cooked to your liking.

Serve with the mint yoghurt sauce.

SERVES 6

When Dirk Bogarde arrived in Hollywood, G befriended him. He called her the Marmalade Aunt since she made marmalade from her citrus trees and called it "the other Cooper's marmalade."

Something you do every year like make marmalade has a reassuring continuity about it. We have two cumquat trees and a lemon and a lime. Cumquats, like other citrus, blossom and fruit at the same time, which always seems magical to me. It's a fiddly, sticky job, cutting up the tiny fruits and separating the pips but the smell is a reward in itself. The process of making marmalade has two steps, first the cut up fruit must be boiled with water with the pips in a muslin bags (a clean piece of a Chux will also do nicely). Then the pips are removed, the mixture brought to the boil again and the sugar added. Then it's boiled until setting point is reached. I use trial and error, if the marmalade doesn't set the first time, bring to the boil again. Twenty minutes "rolling" boil is usually enough for the cumquats. The received wisdom is you need two litres of water and two kilograms of sugar to every kilogram of fruit. If you use a one to one ratio, it makes an intense and sharp marmalade which I prefer. If I'm making Seville marmalade I follow my own version of David Mabey's recipe. My little, old, discoloured Penguin edition falls open, splotched and splattered at just the right page.

David Mabey's dark coarse cut marmalade
(adapted from *The Penguin Book of Jams, Pickles and Chutneys* by David and Rose Mabey, [Penguin, 1975])

1½kg oranges
1 lemon
3½ litres water
3kg sugar
2 tbsp black treacle

Wash the fruit, cut in half and squeeze out the juice and pips. Cut the peel into thick shreds and chop the flesh roughly. Put the pips (tied in a muslin bag), flesh, juice and peel into the water and boil gently for about 2 hours or until the volume is reduced by half and the peel is softened. Remove bags of pips and stir in sugar. When the sugar has dissolved, boil rapidly until setting point is reached. Stir in the treacle.

Put into clean, warm jars and seal.

Sydney

Sydney, mid September 1949. From Joan's letters to her mother-in-law:

> *"In Sydney we were met by a barrage of photographers and lights and interviewers and Robbie did broadcasts and newsreels and we didn't have a moment for the first few days. We found a nice little house to move into, in Wolseley Road, Point Piper. It faces the harbour and the garden leads down to a little more or less private beach so it will be ideal for the children when the weather gets hotter. It's like a small English seaside house — quite comfortable but nothing to spoil. We were lucky to get it for 12 guineas a week (about nine pounds in English money) as furnished houses to rent are almost non-existent here — I am now trying to get some domestic help which also seems non-existent. This hotel (The Australian) is large and gloomy like the Midland Manchester — and fantastically expensive. This is quite a pleasant town — like an English provincial town, the harbour is attractive but not so magnificent as San Francisco and the bridge they are so proud of seems a pathetic little thing compared to the bridges in San Francisco and New York. Last Sunday we drove up the coast to see if we would like to live at any of the seaside places — the beaches are wonderful but all the country is overbuilt with shoddy little bungalows like Shoreham. I have yet to see a really nice house; I*

don't think the Australians have much idea of living comfortably. It's nice to have all the English spring flowers here and the fruit is lovely. I'm afraid the food parcels won't be nearly so good from here — butter and tea are rationed (though quite liberally) and sugar is apparently in short supply and not to be sent out of the country. There seems to be plenty of meat — the Australians eat it in enormous quantities for every meal including breakfast! But milk seems to a bit difficult to get — very odd. Took the children to the zoo today where we saw koala bears and sharks and platypus!"

By October Robert and Joan had been to a ball where Joan judged the dresses with the wife of the Italian ambassador who was "very gay and amusing".

Robert also wrote home about our house in Sydney:

"Now I have found a gardener the garden is looking lovely and full of wonderful hydrangeas and gladioli and roses which grow here all the year round. I lunched at the races with a variety of rather odd people who comprise the society here…they are all very nice but live in a whirl of hangovers and baccarat parties and have never really grown up. The real Australia still eludes us and I suppose always will as long as one is in the big cities.

The weeks seem to fly by now and the hot weather has come and I bathe every day from the lawn, very pleasant — our garden is a sort of park for all the local children who come in to use the slide and rush about which is rather fun for Annabel and Sherry and I'm afraid they will miss it all in Melbourne."

In Sydney, Sherry and I put on a play for Sophie Stewart and her husband Ellis Irving. The story goes that Sherry found me hard to direct. I sang "God Save The King" as a finale.

Sydney was also where Michael Blakemore entered our lives. Robert was having his usual row with the management, JC Williamson's, who he considered lazy with regard to publicity. A young man then came to interview Robert for the Sydney University Magazine. Robert found out that he was the son of a prominent Sydney doctor, expected to follow in his father's footsteps but keener on a life in theatre. Robert made him his Publicity Manager on the spot and when the caravan that was *Edward My Son* moved on to Melbourne, Michael came with us, as Sherry's tutor. Robert encouraged him to try his hand as an actor in England, promising his father to keep an eye on Michael, even if it was likely to be his blind eye. Now the most loved and admired of theatre directors, Michael captured Robert in his autobiography in a portrait that is both physically and psychologically astute.

We got to Melbourne in mid December and had Christmas dinner in the garden.

According to Robert:

"...it wasn't all that hot but it made a change. A very good turkey and pudding and some champagne. The company came to a party in the evening and we fed them and their friends on cold turkey and a delicious ham and raspberries and cream and afterwards played charade. I made them all stop and listen to my Xmas speech or rather talk which I had recorded earlier and which I enjoyed at any rate, it really wasn't bad but not up to (JB) Priestly who seems to have the technique better than anyone and who doesn't sound woebegone which nearly everyone else does. Someone said I sounded homesick and I know what they meant.

Abbie and Sherry have just come back from tea with some English people who have lived here for ten years and still hate it! It is curious what a much nicer place Sydney is — the weather I suppose has a lot to do with it and there are no good restaurants here and the shops pretty feeble. I have had quite a lot of racing and am nearly 250 pounds up which is not bad as I don't bet more than five pounds at a time. I get a lot of information from the owners at the luncheons before the races which are always the same menu: oysters, lobsters, lamb, strawberries and champagne. I have become quite attached to the little house and there are one or two nice trees in the garden and a lawn to sit about on. The children went to a matinee of The Glass Slipper *last week and Abbie came back exhausted having taken the whole thing far too seriously.*

I must say I find Melbourne people a good deal duller than the Sydney ones, they tend to pride themselves on their traditions and are fearfully hidebound. I never stop praising the Labour Government to them in the most extravagant terms and have, I fear, the reputation of being a communist. The election went off very quietly and is now forgotten...I can't imagine why they've chosen Menzies...no one thinks the Liberals will be able to do much with a Labour Senate. The new government here has done nothing at all and is not likely to release petrol or outlaw communism, which were two of their rasher promises.

We had a lovely picnic on Sunday in the country and motored miles until we found a deserted beach to bathe from and then all got stuck in the mud. But enjoyed it v. much.

There's still plenty of meat eaten in Sydney. I don't think you can beat Australian lamb, especially now we are more adventurous in how we cook it and serve it."

This Terry Durack recipe was apparently created because he and his wife Jill Dupleix were starving and couldn't bear to wait the requisite time for a traditional roast leg of lamb.

Easter lamb with garlic and herbs

1 leg of lamb (about 2 kilos)
3 tbsp roughly chopped parsley
4 cloves garlic, crushed
2 anchovies, chopped
2 tbsp capers, drained
1 tbs coarsely grated lemon rind
3 tbsp soft, fresh breadcrumbs
3 tbsp olive oil
4 sprigs rosemary
extra oil for drizzling

Heat oven to 220°C. Hold leg of lamb with fleshiest side towards you and slice directly through the meat four or five times, about 2.5cm apart, almost to the bone as if you were cutting steaks but leaving them attached. Mix parsley, garlic, anchovies, capers, lemon rind and breadcrumbs together and add olive oil to make a mush. Using your hands, push the paste between the slices. Scatter with rosemary sprigs and drizzle with oil. Roast at 220°C for 20 minutes then reduce heat to 190°C for 45 minutes. Remove lamb. Let it rest under foil for 10–15 mins then carve across the joint so everyone gets meat and stuffing.

Serve with roasted potatoes and tomatoes.

SERVES 6

Old Nan holding Sherry, Robert and Joan
photographed by Cecil Beaton, 1942

Robert, Sherry, me and Joan (1947)

Big sister to Will, a sunny chubby baby (1951)

Chapter Four

BIG BROTHER, LITTLE BROTHER

Back from our travels, we settled into a rebuilt "Fairmans", with a large bedroom for my parents and a dressing room and bathroom for my father. He chose the tiles for the bathroom (pink) and the towels (purple). He loved colour. He was one of the first men to wear pink shirts when they became fashionable and he had a very strange mustard yellow suit, which had been made for a film so it had no lining. He wore it once to appear on Michael Parkinson's show. In the car on the way to London, he dropped cigar ash onto it and burnt a large hole in the lapel which he had to hold his hand over for the duration of the interview.

Will

My younger brother Wilton, named for Robert's father the Major was born in August 1951. He was a sunny, chubby baby and I announced "Now I'm a rose between two thorns" when I saw him for the first time. When Will was eight months old a journalist called Margaret Pearson came and wrote an article about us: "At home with Robert Morley, Playwright, Actor and Adoring Father".

> *"Fairman's Cottage which is a pleasant not too large white house has been built in fits and starts, and began originally as a wattle and daub cottage in the sixteenth century. Then it was strengthened with beams and uprights made of old ship's timbers...the house has been altered considerably since the Morleys bought it about twelve years ago, and some of it is very new indeed, as it has been added onto as each new baby came about. The newest room (in honour of Wilton's arrival) is the pleasant white-walled sitting room with ceiling beams to match the old ship's timbers, and a long mantelpiece built to display a gay collection of Staffordshire china. The long windows are framed with warm coloured chintz."*

When the journalist arrived she was apparently:

> *"...escorted inside to find the whole family...sedate Sheridan, loquacious Annabel and the bouncing newcomer, Wilton...engrossed in spring cleaning, with Mrs Morley busy dusting books in the dining room and the small Annabel not yet six and already an experienced actress, busy dusting her intriguing collapsible doll's house which has already been round the world with her. Annabel was called over to say 'How d'you do?'. 'I don't think I will,' she said quite firmly. 'I'm weally wather shy.'"*

I was also asked about the process of filming and described it as "wather boring sometimes, you just sit up there and the men tell you to do this and that."

The family, Mrs Pearson continued:

> *"...lives in the pleasant sitting room and it is there that Sheridan*

(called Sherry by the family) keeps his gramophone and his large pile of records. He already has more than fifty records of his own, it is there too that Annabel keeps her box of comics which she has no difficulty in persuading 'Dardy' to read to her."

My father reported to our grandmother when Will was three and a half that whenever any outing or indeed any activity was suggested he would say enthusiastically, "What fun, do let's." For quite a while he was complicit in all my schemes. I could dress him up and include him in my games. Then, of course, as he got bigger, he lost interest and became involved with his friends and things like go-carting through the woods, and playing with knives, bows and arrows.

Sherry

Will's arrival had made us three.

Sheridan, named for Sheridan Whiteside, the character Robert was playing in *The Man Who Came to Dinner*, was born just before Christmas, 1941. Then my father went away on tour around the provinces. His letters to my mother are full of how much he misses her, how he is going to try and phone so he can hear her voice, how beautiful he thinks she is and how much he loves her and his son, a large healthy baby with rather sticking out ears.

When you have an older sibling you always want to catch up. Deborah Devonshire, the youngest of the six Mitford sisters, called her autobiography *Wait For Me*. My mother lost a baby between Sherry's birth and mine, so Sherry was five when I was born.

A picture taken at that time shows Robert looking in at us through the nursery window. I am in my high chair and Joan is feeding me, Sherry sits at the table looking intently at our mother. Perhaps I am reading too much into his expression but sometimes

I think he must have felt usurped by a younger sister after five years of being an only child. Surely he must have resented having to share his adored mother with a little sister. In another photo, taken at my christening, he stands solemn and watchful, pulling at his coat. Later, when we were in Sydney in 1949 Sherry tried to "direct" me in the entertainment we were putting on and I remember resisting doing anything he said and doing exactly what I wanted to do.

After studying at Oxford, Sherry became a television journalist, a biographer, and finally a theatre critic. Someone asked Robert what it was like to have a son who was a theatre critic. "Like being a high ranking member of the Israeli government and waking up to find your son has become a Palestinian sympathiser," he replied. Robert was less than delighted when Sherry got into Oxford, which Robert thought was a waste of time. This led to a mild row, one of the two rows Sherry and Robert had. The second row, which caused a rift which never entirely healed, was when Sherry left his first wife Margaret, whom he had met at the University of Hawaii where he went to teach after Oxford. They married in Boston, in the mid '60s, because that's where Margaret's family lived and moved to a Berkshire house, a few miles from my parents. Sherry's children Hugo, Alexis and Juliet were born there. Both my parents loved Margaret, so they were less than thrilled when Sherry left her for Ruth Leon. Robert apparently said to Sherry, "One falls in love with people but it's very unwise to leave home for them."

Sherry wrote a great deal about the family, biographies of G and Robert and then his own autobiography. In adulthood he liked to appropriate Robert's anecdotes and re-tell them. He copied Robert's bombast but there was one essential difference; Robert was a listener, fascinated by people and their stories. Sherry on the other hand, was poised when someone else was talking to cut in and cap the story with a better one. His relationship with Will and me was essentially competitive, as if he had to prove that he was the most successful, the best paid, the most responsible. I think Sherry hankered after Robert's fame and recognition and yet Will, to whom those things have never mattered a jot, resembles Robert in his zest for life and his generosity. He grows more and more like him as he gets older. Will is an adoring father of two and his children now sit at the narrow lime-oak "Fairmans" dining room table and grow up surrounded by pictures of us all.

The chocolate thieves

My father and the black cat, Tom, were both addicted to Cadbury's Dairy Milk Chocolate. "The really big bars," my father would say if anyone visiting asked if they could bring something. "It has to be the really big chunky bars." My mother used to hide the chocolate, pushing the bars behind the tins of peaches and sardines and the birthday cake candles in a cupboard in the passage between the hall and the sitting room. But Robert and Tom would go on a rampage and sniff out the hiding place.

Dark chocolate is best for cooking; I don't bother with the really fancy stuff. Always melt chocolate in a bowl over a saucepan of simmering water and don't stir it until it has melted. You will never find me making anything which includes white chocolate, I hate the sickly after taste. In fact I find anything made with chocolate *can* be a bit sickly. I usually add a dash of coffee to brownies, both in the batter and the icing. Of course, you don't need to do this if you have made the brownie syrup below because it already has coffee in it. These brownies are my signature dish, or as near to a signature dish as I'll ever come. I must have been making them since I was about 12 or 13 and have adapted the recipe over time. No other recipe I have found has ever come close to this one. I don't like nuts in my brownies and I do like them iced.

Chocolate brownies

    200g butter
    200g brown sugar
    3 eggs
    250g dark chocolate (cooking chocolate is fine) melted over hot water
    60g plain flour (you can add more flour for a firmer, more "cakey" consistency)
    2 tsp vanilla essence
    pinch of salt
    2 dessertspoons syrup (see recipe below)

SYRUP

    200g caster sugar
    100ml coffee
    1 dessertspoon of cocoa
    1 tsp cornflour

ICING

    1 tbs castor sugar
    1 tbs cocoa
    125g butter

Cream butter and sugar, add eggs, one at a time, stir in melted chocolate, sieved flour, salt and vanilla. Mix well. Stir in the syrup.

For syrup: Boil sugar and coffee together for 5 minutes and add cocoa and cornflour. Bring to boil again. This will keep in a screw top jar in the fridge.

Bake in a baking-paper-lined tin (23cm square) at 180°C for 20–30 minutes. Brownies should be firm but still a little gooey in the middle.

I ice them as soon as they come out of the oven. I ice the brownies in the pan, then refrigerate until firm before cutting into squares.

To make the icing: mix sugar, cocoa, butter and a little water in a saucepan. Bring to the boil and simmer until thick. You can use this just as it is, like a glaze, or mix in some icing sugar to make a thicker consistency.

MAKES A 23CM SQUARE PAN FULL

This is another delicious chocolate treat. It is very rich, so tiny slices go well with coffee. However, it freezes well.

Truffle terrine

- ½ cup raisins
- 2 tbsp rum
- ½ cup slivered almonds, toasted
- ½ cup glacé apricots, diced
- 2 cups Amaretti biscuits
- 250g dark chocolate
- 200g softened butter
- 2 tsp icing sugar
- ½ cup cocoa
- 2 egg yolks

Grease a 23x8cm oblong loaf tin. Soak raisins in rum for 2 hours. Put almonds, apricots and Arametti biscuits, broken into crumbs, in a bowl and mix, add raisins and rum. Mix well and set aside while you make the chocolate base.

Melt chocolate and butter over hot water. Stir in icing sugar, cocoa and egg yolks, combine well and then mix into fruit and biscuit mixture. Turn out into the loaf pan and smooth down. Tap sharply to make sure mixture goes into the corners of the tin. Cover with foil and refrigerate overnight.

To unmould: Plunge tin into shallow sink of hot water for a few seconds, then turn upside down onto a flat plate. Smooth over with a palate knife. Cut into thin slices with a sharp knife.

SERVES 8–10

One of our favourite London restaurants was Prunier's. Madame Prunier kept going all through World War II and was still running the restaurant with a rod of iron in the 1950s. It was a fish restaurant, so perfect for my mother who always had melon followed by Dover sole and then a petit pot du chocolate.

Petit pots du chocolate

250g dark chocolate, finely chopped
50gm (½ cup) cocoa
2 egg yolks
60g caster sugar
250ml pouring cream
250ml milk

Melt chocolate and stir in cocoa. Whisk sugar and egg yolks until pale. Bring milk and cream to the boil and gradually add first egg yolk mixture then chocolate, stirring to incorporate. Divide among four 200ml cups or pots and refrigerate until set.

SERVES 4

Gypsies

One day when the boys and I were being taken on our usual walk down the long straight road which led to Wargrave village we met a gypsy caravan, pulled by a rather reluctant pony — traditional gypsy caravans are enormously heavy. On the door were the names Sheridan, Annabel and Wilton, and inside was Robert, beaming. Gypsy caravans were traditionally burnt when the family line dies out, but Robert had come across one and had it repainted. Inside it had an extraordinarily clever use of space; lockers and cupboards for storage, a bed which pulled out on runners and a cupboard which opened up underneath for two or three generations' sleeping space. There was even a glass-fronted cupboard in which I put my doll's tea set. It had an outside larder, like a wire meat safe for storing food. Gypsies were a common feature in my childhood, they arrived in spring or early summer and camped on the common at the top of Crazies Hill and the women came door-to-door selling clothes' pegs.

ABBIE WITH SNOWY THE CAT, WILL AND ROBERT

Buck, G and Joan (1919)

G as I remember her

Chapter Five

BUCK'S CLUB AND REGATTA TEAS

My mother's parents were Herbert Buckmaster and Gladys Cooper. My father's father died before I was born and I have only dim memories of Robert's mother Gertrude (Daisy) Fass. Gladys, who we always called G and Buck, on the other hand, featured very strongly in my childhood.

My father, Robert, loved food, indeed he was consoled by it. He was also adventurous and had high standards, although he loved a boiled egg with brown bread and butter as much as he loved foie gras. It was his delight in food that made me into a cook, briefly a caterer, and my brother into the restaurateur that he is; although Wilton would probably say he has modelled himself on our grandfather, Buck of Buck's Club.

Robert introduced two generations, his children and his grandchildren, to restaurant dining. My first experience of eating in a restaurant was in Buck's Club, 18 Clifford Street, off Bond Street, London. Although the club itself was strictly members (men) only, there was a Ladies' Annex, converted from the premises at the back which had been a flower shop. Here members could take their wives, girlfriends or daughters to eat the same food as the members. It must be remembered that gentleman's club food is essentially English nursery food (give or take a few small game birds).

As a small child, if I was taken to London to the dentist or to buy new clothes or shoes, I was also taken to lunch at Buck's. The menu always included a chicken pâté, covered by a layer of clarified butter in which had been placed two bay leaves. This was served in a shallow oblong white china dish. It consisted of about eight portions of wonderfully smooth rich pâté. The first time this was ordered for me I imagined I had to eat the whole thing. My mother was momentarily distracted and I was about halfway through and turning green when she realised and whipped the dish away.

Here's my version, simplicity itself and as full of taste as homemade dishes can be.

Chicken liver pâté

1 small onion
butter for frying
250g chicken livers (larger ones to be cut in half)
pinch of thyme
1–2 tbsp sherry or port
1–2 tbsp cream (to taste)
butter (extra)

Chop onion and fry in butter until soft. Add cleaned chicken livers. Season well with salt and pepper and add thyme. Cook gently until the livers are firm but still pink inside. Remove from the pan and process or liquidise. Deglaze the pan with sherry or port and add to mixture with cream. Keep a bit of texture in the mixture. Scrape pâté into a bowl, melt some more butter in the same pan and pour over the surface. Place in the refrigerator until set.

Serve with hot toast and some cornichons.

The following terrine is a bit more work but is excellent. It is better made a few days ahead so the flavours can develop.

Terrine

>   600g chicken livers
>   6 tbsp port
>   pinch of thyme
>   2 bay leaves, crumbled (and more to decorate)
>   4 slices ham
>   350g sausage meat
>   3 slices white bread, soaked in a little milk
>   ½ clove garlic, crushed150ml dry white wine
>   8–10 thin rashers of streaky bacon

Place the chicken livers in a bowl, add the port, thyme and two of the bay leaves. Allow to marinate for at least 2 hours. Put ¾ of the livers into a food processor and add the ham, sausage meat, bread and garlic. Season well with salt and pepper. Process, adding white wine to make a rather wet mixture. Line a loaf tin with the bacon rashers. Spread half the mixture in the tin, add the remaining whole chicken livers in a layer, then cover with the remaining mixture. Top with more bacon rashers and bay leaves.

Place in a Bain Marie and cook at 180°C for 75–90 minutes. Remove from oven. Place a weight on top so the juices can run out and refrigerate.

SERVES: 8–10 SLICES

At Buck's there were two waitresses, Rose and Connie, who always looked to me like old fashioned parlour maids in their white caps and aprons. One night when Robert and Buck were in the Ladies' Annex quite late Connie came through to say there was only one member left in the Members' rooms. Buck told her to go home and said he'd lock up the premises. He then asked who the late guest was. Connie replied that it was Mr Macmillan. My father suggested Connie give Macmillan the keys and ask him to lock the front door when he left and drop the keys back through the letter box. However, Buck doubted he could be trusted to do that properly. My father replied that he *was* the Prime Minister. Even so, Buck thought, it was better he do it himself!

Buck's had a fearsome cook, the only person who could make my grandfather nervous. She was called Mrs Hillsden and was rather like Mrs Bridges in *Upstairs, Downstairs* or the cook in *Gosford Park*. After lunch my brother Sheridan and I would be taken down to Mrs Hillsden's basement kitchen where we would shake her hand and say "Thank you for my nice lunch."

In the 1920s the Irish barman at the club, Pat McGarry, invented the cocktail "Buck's Fizz": orange juice, champagne and a mystery ingredient. Even without the mystery ingredient, a Buck's Fizz is delicious. Buck would spin in his grave at the thought of using anything but freshly squeezed orange juice and a decent champagne.

The sort of food Buck's served, still does perhaps, was the food the members had grown up eating — comfort food. When it is well cooked from the best ingredients, there is nothing nicer. Unfortunately the boarding school versions were frequently some of the most disgusting. Congealing tapioca pudding, lumpy custard and gristly chops are only some of the things that have contributed to giving English food a bad name.

However, chicken fricassee is the best sort of nursery fare and a good way of using up a cold roast chicken.

Chicken fricassee

This is simply largish pieces of roasted or poached chicken in a béchamel sauce.

>leftover roasted or poached chicken (1/2 a chicken)
>250–300g asparagus or broccoli
>½ cup coarse breadcrumbs
>½ tbsp butter or olive oil or a mixture for frying the breadcrumbs
>1 clove garlic, crushed
>1 tbs parsley, chopped

BÉCHAMEL SAUCE
>50g butter
>2–3 tbsp plain flour
>pinch of salt
>2 cups milk or half and half milk and chicken stock
>dash of Noilly Prat or any dry white vermouth

Steam asparagus or broccoli and layer it in the bottom of a deep dish. Add chicken on top, cut or torn into large pieces and cover with sauce.

To make the sauce: Melt butter and add flour and salt. Stir in the milk and cook until thickened.

Season well with salt and pepper. Top with the rustic breadcrumbs, lightly fried with garlic and parsley. Cook at 180°C for 30–45 minutes or until everything is piping hot.

Serve with rice and a green salad.

SERVES 4

Buck and G

Herbert Buckmaster was G's first husband. She was 18 and performing in a musical called *Havana* in 1907 when she eloped to marry him, thus becoming the black sheep of the family. Buck was already the black sheep of his family and working as a bookmaker, a profession his clergyman father strongly disapproved of. G was a Gaiety Girl, a sort of chorus girl, not yet on the legitimate stage. Buck was what was called "a stage-door Johnnie", a young man who hung around the stage door, waiting to take the prettiest girls out to supper at Romano's. They married and had my mother, Joan in 1910 and my uncle, Johnnie in 1915. Buck had been a soldier in the Boer War and when the First World War started he was keen to enlist. G had previously met Lord Birkenhead, a big cheese in the War Office so she went to see him to try and get a commission for Buck. Birkenhead was in his office, with his secretary, Winston Churchill when G was shown in. She announced she'd come for a job. The two men roared with laughter. "For yourself?" Birkenhead asked. "No, for my husband," G explained.

So by 1915 Buck was in France, in the trenches. On the eve of his departure, his father-in-law wrote him a most touching letter, expressing his "…earnest hope that you will come back safely to those whom we all love". G sent Buck parcels: clean linen, a periscope, apples and pears, Dundee cakes, gaiters, toothpowder, jam puddings and Devonshire cream. While he was in the trenches Buck conceived the idea for a man's club for officers and gentlemen.

Unfortunately their marriage did not survive the war. While Buck was away in France, G became co-manager of the Playhouse Theatre, near Charing Cross station. She said running the Playhouse was the happiest time of her life. When war broke out she was earning £20 a week, when it ended she was earning £4000 a year. In 1918 alone she made £5000 as a share of the Playhouse's profit.

Buck came back to someone used to doing without him, someone used to managing her own life. She had an entirely new set of friends and so did he. Buck said he loathed the idea of divorce and not being able to see his children grow up but in fact the divorce was managed very amicably and Buck remained very much in his children's lives. He always said of G that "No children ever had a better mother than Joan and John."

Both G and Buck remarried twice more but remained fond of each other. Buck was G's greatest fan. He was outraged when her second husband Neville Pearson divorced her. He said, "I always knew he was a cad and a bounder."

Buck was a small, shortish man with white hair and a moustache, always immaculately dressed. If he came to stay at weekends he wore a silk scarf as a cravat with his dressing gown. When Buck got very old and his arthritis was giving him great pain he came to live with us. About 11am he would start getting restless and if my father wasn't there to offer him the first of two massive dry martinis he would become increasingly bad tempered. When he'd had the first, a small glass full of gin, a twist of lemon peel and drop of Noilly Prat, he'd say "I don't mind if I have the other half." This fascinated me, the other half of what, I'd wonder. He also taught me that it was very rude to say to someone "Would you like another drink?" since this implied that they'd had one or more already.

At some point Buck had owned a yacht and as he lay dying he imagined he was back on the yacht. "Ready to cast off?" he'd ask visitors to his bedroom and wonder aloud why they weren't suitably dressed and wearing their plimsolls. He had a tattoo on each forearm, which fascinated me as a very little girl. I wondered how the pictures stayed on. One was of an anchor and the other was a Tudor Rose. As a very little girl he called me "Canary Top" and I named my canary "Bertie" after him. Of course no one called him Bertie or Herbert, he was always Buck.

G was as unlike my other grandmother, Daisy, as it was possible to be. Daisy was a Victorian, or at least an Edwardian figure, who wore long, dark shapeless clothes, walked with a stick and often took to her bed. Known as poor Daisy, because of her unsatisfactory husband, my gambler grandfather, she always seemed faintly disapproving.

G was a great beauty in her youth and she remained a great beauty all her life. At the height of her popularity hundreds and hundreds of picture postcards of her in every conceivable outfit from full evening dress to sou'westers and oilskins to tennis gear were sold and eagerly collected. In the First World War soldiers decorated their billets with them and went into battle with packets of postcards in the breast pockets of their uniforms; once such a wad of postcards deflected a German bullet and saved a soldier's life. We know this because his widow sent the postcards to my mother when my grandmother died.

Gladys was very amused when Buck told her the men pinned her pictures and postcards up in their billets. When Buck arrived in France with the Royal Horseguards he passed a dugout and heard one man say to another "Buckmaster's come out." The reply was "As 'e brought Gladys Cooper with 'im?"

One of Buck's duties was to censor the men's letters home. One wrote "We've got a new troop officer out here, Gladys Cooper's husband. He's not a bad sort but in no way conspicuous for his good looks." "I suppose," wrote Buck, "as Gladys Cooper's husband, they expected me to be a sort of Apollo Belvedere."

From *Buck's Book* (Grayson and Grayson, 1933).

After her career as an actress-manager, G married for a second time to a rich, handsome newspaper magnate, produced my aunt Sally, and lived in some style as Lady Pearson in 1 and 2 The Grove, Highgate (a house much later lived in by Sting). When that marriage ended she fell in love with an actor, Philip Merivale, and took on his four children. She went to America, acted on Broadway, and then auditioned for Hitchcock's *Rebecca*. She got the part (as Laurence Olivier's sensible sister, Beatrice) and moved to California.

G in America

California is where we met, in 1948 when I was three and she was 61. Tall, blonde, tanned, dressed usually in a pair of shorts and a sun top, she swam (naked) in her pool, gardened, shopped and drove at a ferocious pace. She was unsentimental, practical, brave, a "looks" snob and elegant in the kind of casual clothes she favoured. She wore the trousers in every sense. She called me "Princess", stuck a hibiscus flower behind her ear and put one behind mine. Our relationship was as sunny as the Californian weather, one of mutual adoration and approval. Her house in Napoli Drive, Pacific Palisades had a garden of citrus trees, oranges, lemons and grapefruit, from which she made marmalade. In London she had acted with Seymour Hicks and Gerald du Maurier, followed by another generation, Laurence Olivier, Paul Schofield and Kay Kendall and yet still another, Vanessa Redgrave. Plays were written for her by Somerset Maugham and Noel Coward. In Hollywood films she played tight-lipped, cruel mothers (*Now, Voyager*), the exasperated mother of Professor Henry Higgins (*My Fair Lady*), a Mother Superior (*The Song of Bernadette*), and plain, discarded wives (Lady Nelson in *That Hamilton Woman*). She was playing Mrs Medlock, the unsympathetic housekeeper in *The Secret Garden* when we stayed with her in 1949. Like several great beauties I have known, she took very little account of her looks. They had been her luck and what got her into the theatre but for years they stopped her being taken seriously as an actress. She said her best notice was an early one: "Gladys Cooper surprised us."

By the time my brother Wilton was born in the early 50s, G

had bought a house in Oxfordshire in Henley on Thames about five miles from our house, "Fairmans". Henley was much more raffish and sophisticated than our village with its trippers who came in charabancs and strolled along the tow path eating ice-creams. To get into Henley you crossed an old stone bridge with a head of Father Thames, a pagan River God with flowing hair and beard, who looked like God the Father, on one side, and Mother Thames on the other. Henley had restaurants and cafes and shops and a cinema. It had a grocer's, much grander than Wargrave's International Stores, where my mother bought coffee, lump sugar and tins of tongue (a particular favourite of Robert's). G's house "Barn Elms" was the only private house on the Regatta Course. It was a weatherboard house with a veranda and the same indoor-outdoor feel as the house in Pacific Palisades. The French windows onto the veranda were always open; in winter when the fire was blazing and the central heating blasting she would still have the windows thrown open. At the bottom of the garden a line of huge chestnut trees screened the house from the tow path.

After Wilton arrived I was no longer the adored youngest grandchild and my relationship with G began to suffer. One afternoon she drove me to see some dogs she had in kennels near Henley. (Her dogs, usually yappy corgis, were transported back and forth across the Atlantic with her as she travelled). On the way back, sighing, I said I hadn't enjoyed the excursion much. G pointed out she hadn't promised me anything much; she'd only asked if I'd care to see the dogs and I had said I would. There was silence after that until, passing through Henley, G saw swans on the river and decided to feed them. "We haven't time," I said, "we must get back to tea." "We've plenty of time," said G. "In any case," I said, "we haven't got food for the swans." "I'm going to buy some stale bread from that baker's on the corner," said G and she did.

When she came out of the shop with the bag of stale bread in her hand, I asked if I could have it. On being told I couldn't, I pleaded hunger. "Nonsense," said G, "you don't want stale bread, you'll be having your nice tea in a minute." "But I'm so terribly hungry," I said, turning the tears full on. When I saw that my grandmother had no intention of giving way, I sobbed: "But it happens to be my favourite food. Oh, how can you take my favourite food away from me!" Though she pretended to take no notice, G secretly thought this was not a bad performance, tears and all.

For several years after this we engaged in what Robert called "The Cold War". We only communicated through a third party: "Ask Abbie if she wants some cake", G would say. "Tell Granny, I'll have a piece of the orange one." She had a will of iron but so, aged about six, did I. She was stubborn, convinced she was in the right and so was I. We both enjoyed the theatricality of it but when we eventually made up, we were ever afterwards firm friends.

Henley

On the Saturday of Regatta week, the first week in July, G always gave a party, starting in the afternoon so people could watch the races on the river and continuing until the celebratory fireworks which marked the end of the Regatta. The great attraction for us as children — since the idea of men rowing up and down the river was, if anything, even more boring than Wimbledon, which half the guests would be watching on TV with the curtains drawn — was the funfair. For years this took place in the field next to G's house.

One memorable night there was a "rumble", a fight between the local Teddy Boys and the fairground men. Someone from the fair was knifed. He was brought to G's house and she rang for the ambulance. The matriarch of the fairground family was a middle aged woman with brassy dyed blonde hair who performed her snake act dressed in a leopard-skin two-piece costume. She pulled pythons from a battered green wooden box where they lay snuggled in old army blankets. She wrapped them round her body and, as the finale, placed a flickering-tongued head in her mouth. Perhaps this matriarch was the mother or the grandmother of the young man who was knifed because the reward for G's good deed was that we got to go on any fairground ride and in to see the snake lady's act for free.

G, like my mother, didn't make cakes but she searched out interesting breads from local bakeries. I remember a delicious malt bread called Harvo. She also used to buy an orange cake which was a big flattish sponge cake, baked in a fluted edged tin, with an orange filling and a glacé icing studded with pieces of candied peel.

This recipe is for a tea bread which is actually made with tea.

Farmhouse teabread

25g diced mixed peel
50g raisins
50g sultanas
finely grated zest of 2 oranges
1 tsp cinnamon
½ tsp all spice
325ml freshly brewed tea
1 egg
200g brown sugar
275g self raising flour

Put peel, raisins, sultanas, orange zest and spices in a large bowl, mix and pour over tea. Cover and leave for several hours. Beat egg lightly and add to mixing bowl with sugar. Sift on flour and beat until all ingredients are well blended. Pour into a lined loaf tin and bake at 180°C for 1¾ hours.

Serve sliced and spread with butter.

MAKES ONE LOAF

G would have approved of this banana bread, full of good things.

Wholemeal banana bread

    1½ cups wholemeal flour
    2 tsp baking powder
    ½ cup wheatgerm
    ½ cup skim milk powder
    1 tsp cinnamon
    2 large bananas, mashed
    grated zest of 1 orange
    60ml macadamia oil
    2 eggs
    ½ cup maple syrup or honey
    2 tsp vanilla essence
    ½ cup chopped dried apricots
    150g blueberries, fresh or frozen

Combine flour, baking powder, wheatgerm, skim milk powder and cinnamon in a large bowl. In another bowl combine mashed bananas with orange zest, oil, eggs, maple syrup and vanilla. Fold banana mixture into flour mixture, add apricots and blueberries. Mix well. Pour into a lined loaf tin and bake at 175°C for 50 minutes. Serve sliced as is or toasted with more blueberries, sliced bananas and maple syrup.

MAKES ONE LOAF

G often served cucumber sandwiches for tea and said this was how Chekhov had liked them.

Chekhovian cucumber sandwiches

> bread, thinly-sliced
> butter
> cucumber
> salt and pepper
> pinch of sugar
> mint, finely chopped

Butter thinly-sliced brown bread (butter is essential, margarine simply will not do). Cover with very thinly sliced, peeled cucumber. Sprinkle with salt, pepper and a little sugar. Add a generous quantity of very finely chopped mint. Cut off the crusts and cut sandwiches into two or three "fingers".

I still think of cucumber sandwiches being quintessentially English. Think of the butler Lane in *The Importance of Being Earnest* lamenting the dearth of cucumbers in the market, when they were not available "even for ready money".

The first things I ever cooked were cakes, from packets brought over by G from the States: Betty Crocker and Mary Baker, Devil's Food and Angel's Food — all one did was add an egg and water.

This cake is like the orange cakes G used to buy.

Orange cake

> 125g butter
> ¾ cup sugar

2 eggs
1½ cups self raising flour
¼ cup orange juice
¼ cup mixed peel

ORANGE ICING
175g softened butter
250g sifted icing sugar
grated rind and juice of 1 orange

Beat butter and sugar, add eggs one at a time. Add sifted flour and orange juice and beat together. Add mixed peel. Bake in a greased ring tin at 190°C for 35 minutes.

To make the icing beat butter and icing sugar together, gradually adding orange juice until you have the right consistency.

G was someone who was never ill and never even took so much as an aspirin. Although she strongly disapproved of Edith Evans' Christian Science beliefs, G was virtually in accordance with them. "Mind over matter" was one of her creeds and complaining of a cold or a headache to her was met with absolutely no sympathy at all. When she was in her early eighties and touring around England in a revival of *The Chalk Garden* she developed a terrible cough and was diagnosed with viral pneumonia. She was also diagnosed with lung cancer although this latter diagnosis was kept from her. She had long been a smoker of Turkish cigarettes, made to her specification.

She was discharged from hospital to die at home in her bedroom overlooking the garden at "Barn Elms", the towpath and the river. Our wonderful family doctor, Joe Paton, was in attendance and gave her a shot of morphine daily. "I don't know what Joe injects me with" she reported to my father, "but I must say I do rather look forward to it." She would have been horrified had she known it was morphine.

G lived to 81. She got out of bed on the last evening of her life (by then there was a nurse in attendance) and walked over to her dressing table to make up that famous face. "Really," she said, "if this is what viral pneumonia does to the complexion, I shan't bother to have it again." That night she died in her sleep. They dimmed the lights along Shaftesbury Avenue.

G's funeral was wonderful. As the floral tributes arrived I read out to my mother the names on the cards, for her to make a list. "Betty, Betty?" she queried. Then looking at the card attached to a huge heart-shaped arrangement of red roses, "Oh, Bette Davis," she said.

After G's funeral, which took place in Remenham church we all sat in her sitting room, unable to believe that she wasn't about to stride in, whistling her tuneless little whistle. At her funeral we had sung both *The Battle Hymn of the Republic* and *To Be A Pilgrim*. The first line of which is: "He who would valiant be..." Valiant is a good choice of adjective for G. To have brought up children while working in the theatre, to have made a career in the theatre when it was not really considered a suitable profession for a young woman, to have taught herself to be a good, even sometimes a great actress. To have had great fame and not let it turn her head, to have been a hard worker all her life and yet not let that job take precedence over the importance of family and friends. Acting was to G, like it was to my father, a job. You went out and did it, you didn't agonise over it or give it undue importance and when the performance was over, you went home. Her houses, her children and grandchildren, her dogs and all the other animals she collected and loved, sunshine, gardens, those were the things that mattered.

She was once having lunch with Robert and the police rang to tell her that her London flat had been broken into and all her jewellery had been stolen, none of it insured. "What will you do?" asked my father. "Have another cup of coffee, I think," said G. Valiant.

The recipes in this chapter remind me of G and those "Barn Elms" teas: on the veranda on a summer afternoon, the River Thames at the bottom of the garden and G presiding over the tea table, bossing her deaf sister Gracie about and getting her to fetch more cups. Gracie, being Gracie, would ignore G. There would be a dog or two lying at our feet, waiting for a discarded sandwich crust or half a biscuit. My beautiful aunt Sally and her little girls would be there, my step aunt Rosamond and her girls would arrive. At one time there was even an old rowing boat someone energetic might take out on the river, and if it was a Sunday local actors might arrive, Bea Lillie, Roland Culver and Celia Johnson. If my grandfather Buck was staying with us, he would come too and he and G would reminisce about old friends and their shared past as they ate cucumber sandwiches and orange cake.

G, SHERRY AND JOAN – TEA ON THE LAWN MID 1940S

Chapter Six

NEIGHBOURS AND WEEKEND GUESTS

Our immediate neighbours were the Bushes who farmed across the road, Joe Paton the doctor and his family who lived diagonally opposite, and the Hearns, who lived just down the road a little. Peter Hearn, the farmer's son, married a beautiful exotic Iranian girl he met at Agricultural College. When the Shah's regime fell, Jaleh's father was imprisoned and she had hair-raising stories of her (eventually successful) efforts to get him released. My father adored her and not only because Jaleh's chickens produced the most wonderful eggs; whenever he returned from being away the first meal was always a "Jaleh" boiled egg with brown bread and butter.

Eggs are the most alchemical of ingredients; rather like a very versatile actor they can be anything you like from breakfast's poached or scrambled, through to the soufflé, meringue or mousse of a dinner party.

I made the raspberry hazelnut meringue (below) when Charlie and I were in New Zealand; Robert was doing *How The Other Half Loves* there in 1976 and he gave Charlie a part in it. Will was the company manager and stunned us all by marrying a beautiful flight attendant, just before the family arrived in NZ. Charlie and I had a party and I made this, with great effort, grinding the hazelnuts in a coffee grinder and beating the egg whites by hand. I put it on the kitchen bench and went to the theatre. When we came home a trail of ants were traversing the kitchen. I rushed to rescue the meringues. "No good," said Charlie regretfully, "they've moved in and had their babies." Indeed ants were entering one side of the meringues and exiting the other like old drunks reeling out of a pub.

Raspberry hazelnut meringue

4 egg whites
250g castor sugar
1 dessertspoon of white vinegar
1 tsp vanilla
250g hazelnuts, ground
300ml cream
250g raspberries

Beat egg whites until stiff peaks form. Gradually beat in sugar to make a meringue. Stir in vinegar and vanilla. Fold in ground hazelnuts. Cook in two lined sandwich tins for about 30 minutes at 180°C until the meringue has risen and has a crust on it. Cool then turn out carefully and sandwich together with whipped cream and raspberries. You can also make a raspberry coulis to serve with the meringue cake.

SERVES 6–8

A little further away from us was a large Victorian house called "Maplecroft". I remember going to "Maplecroft" as a little girl when a Mrs Llewellyn lived there with her two daughters. It was a gloomy house then and the inside was dark-brown. In the 1960s Dave Allen, the comedian, and his wife Judith Stott bought it. Judy transformed the house. I particularly remember that she made a Victorian nursery with a doll's house and a rocking horse, everything was white. Dave had a wonderful little circular study-library. As well as Judy's son Jonathan, by her first husband Jeremy Burnham, Dave and Judy had a daughter and a son. When a friend of Judy's died young, the Allens also took on her two daughters.

Judy had been in a play Robert put on when he was in management, a rather risqué comedy about two young men who shared a girlfriend; Judy played the girl. She had also played Laurel, the problem grandchild in *The Chalk Garden*, first with Edith Evans and then with G as Mrs St Maugham. There was something of the eternal child about Judy; she wore navy pleated skirts and sailor collared tops and her blonde hair was cut in a bob. She was like the Pied Piper and visiting children were always encouraged to stay. Judy loved entertaining and the house was often filled with friends and their children. However, my father noted that the only time Dave ever looked really cheerful was when he was waving guests goodbye.

One Christmas Eve the Allens brought a couple who were their house guests to "Fairmans" for a drink. The man sat slumped on our large sofa, monosyllabic and downing whiskies. I remember thinking he had a drunk's bulbous red-veined nose. Only when they left did the penny drop — the boring drunk was Robert Stephens, the greatest actor of his generation, whose beauty in the 1960s had made me reel from a theatre after seeing him as Atahualpa in *The Royal Hunt of the Sun*. The red-headed wife was not Maggie Smith but his then partner, a nice doctor.

On another Christmas we went to the Allens for a drink. Judy's rather forbidding mother from Oxford sat one side of the fireplace and Dave's mother from Ireland, equally disapproving, sat on the other. "How clever of you to have found a matching pair," Robert said to Dave, who merely rolled his eyes.

Once we had a swimming pool we had plenty of visiting families, at least in the summer. Robert wrote of how he would be sitting by the pool and would hear a car door slam, a noise he had come to dread, because it disturbed his afternoon siesta.

"It could be the butcher's car in the drive or the postman's (mysteriously, we still rate two deliveries a day) or it could be my wife back from shopping, only I know she hasn't gone shopping. I close my eyes for the last ten seconds of bliss, and open them, aware of the advance of the Pool Men. They come armed with flippers and rings and inflatable rubber monsters. Some of them even bring aqualungs and snorkel tubes. Some of them are already in swimming costumes, others disappear briefly into the house in search of a changing room and a loo. The mothers, the au pairs, the house guests bring up the rear carrying baskets of food and clothes. Even if one doesn't have to rise to greet the children, it's a brave man who doesn't bestir himself when the grown-ups start introducing each other.

'We've come to swim, I do hope you don't mind. This is Mrs Armitage, who's staying with us, and you know Bertha from Stockholm. George, say good afternoon to Mr Morley. And Prudence. And this is their friend Simon and his friend Tiger, at least we call him Tiger.'

The children approach warily, anxious to have done with formality. They hurry away to dip their hands in the water and look reproachfully at me.

'It's colder than yesterday. Much colder.'

'It's been raining,' I tell them apologetically. Why the hell do I have to apologise for the rainfall?

The largest child always jumps in beside me.

'Not to splash', comes a split second after the soaking.

'I am not sure whether Tiger swims or not,' says one of the mums cheerfully, 'but we shall no doubt find out.'

The mums don't swim, at least not right away. They like to talk and cover themselves with oil. One or two of them bring pencils and The Times *crossword. The children demand an audience. 'Watch me, Mummy, watch me' they shout and Mummy not only watches but shouts back. She knows Sylvia can't hear under her bathing cap so she shouts first to indicate that she wishes to communicate, and the second time, when Sylvia has temporarily disengaged her cap from her ear, because everyone else is shouting too.*

After a few minutes the withdrawal symptoms start. Some of the young begin to shiver violently, some of the mothers to try and get their loved ones out of the water and into a towel. The exchanges begin with cajolery and finish in violent confrontation.

'Mummy says out, Roger. Daphne dear, I think you have been in long enough.' No child ever agrees. It is a point of honour to demand another few minutes, a last float to see who is shivering the most. 'If you don't come out now, I shan't bring you again.' Oh, if only I could believe it, if only Henry believed it, if only Mother herself believed it. 'If you don't come out now there'll be no television for a week.' The threats are empty .They always were, even in my own childhood. When the bathing finally stops, the children begin to think of things for me to do. 'Uncle Robert, will you get the croquet mallets? Mr Morley, will you put up the swing? Can we see the skull which laughs? Where's the cat?'

'You are not to bother Mr Morley,' the mothers insist. 'It's time for tea. I wonder if you have such a thing as a knife. We don't seem to have remembered one for the cake.'

On my way back from the kitchen, I observe little groups picnicking on the grass. I am filled with remorse at my own inhospitality. 'There's food in the house', I tell them, 'and chocolate biscuits and Coca Cola, and I can boil a kettle. It's no trouble.' Before I know what I'm saying we are all in the front garden. Only then do I discover I have already eaten the last Bath Oliver and we're out of bread.

When it's time to go home, everyone comes and thanks me and I beg them to come again, whenever they would like to. I even urge the parents to make a plan for tomorrow, insist next time they come they bring even more of their friends and neighbours. Why, why?"

From *Morley Marvels* by Robert Morley (Barnes and Co, 1979), pp. 22–23.

My parents mostly entertained at weekends; I came across a French expression recently, *l'ami du maison* (literally: the friend of the house) meaning the person everyone in the family is pleased to see, who gives everyone some special part of themselves and leaves with everyone wishing they could stay for longer. The writer Sewell Stokes played this part in our lives. He was Sherry's godfather but to me Sewell, "mad uncle Hamlet" to my "dotty Ophelia", was the perfect adult.

A journalist once noted that Robert spoke to his (baby) son in the same reasoned tones as he spoke to adults. Sewell also spoke to everyone in the same calm, witty way; rather like Colonel Pickering in *My Fair Lady*, he treated flower girls like duchesses. As a guest he needed no special entertainment, he just fitted in with whatever we were all doing. My father often took himself off to write in the mornings in the Colt House so unless Sewell and he were co-writing something, that was my time with Sewell. We painted together, laboriously filling in watercolour illustrations in a series of painting books which were of costumes through the ages. A particular favourite was the medieval one which had men in parti-coloured hose and women in those huge, extraordinary horned headdresses — think *Les Très Riches Heures du Duc du Berry*. The Victorian one was pretty good too, women in crinolines the size of small tents, swagged and ribboned and ruched; lots of opportunity for painting with a very small brush.

Sewell arrived on Friday evenings with a zippered tartan bag; he usually travelled light. He always wore versions of the same clothes: a suit or a sports jacket and trousers, a shirt and tie. In summer he took the jacket off and rolled his shirt sleeves up. He shaved with an old fashioned cut throat razor and a badger's hair brush. When he shaved in the morning, I was allowed to watch. I don't remember ever watching, or indeed wanting to watch, my father shave. As someone who liked to do things with the least possible effort, Robert would have been using an electric razor as soon as they were invented.

Sewell and I went for walks, talking endlessly about everything and anything. When I was perhaps 12 or 13, we walked to the top of Crazies Hill and sat on a bench there to get our breath back and he told me about having been Isadora Duncan's lover in the south of France in the 1920s. Robert always said it was going to bed with Isadora which had put Sewell off heterosexual sex! Sewell's biography of Isadora formed the basis for Karel Reiz's (a great friend of Sewell's) film about the dancer. Isadora was played by Vanessa Redgrave. Another great friend of Sewell's was Ralph Brinton, a designer and Sewell divided his weekends between his friends.

But Sewell always came to us at Christmas. He came:

"... bringing the champagne and the cigars, and obediently placing them on the pile under the tree. I sometimes used to wonder what it was that always brought him to us, always by train and always on Christmas Eve, to share in the ritual of noise and crackers, turkey, plum pudding, decorations, excitement and love. I told myself it was

love but it was also of course custom. Sewell was a creature of custom, the custom all his life of reading and writing and spending hours in the reading room of the Museum and on buses to visit Bully (Peter Bull, Sherry's other godfather) in the King's Road or sometimes to more mysterious friends in Hampstead whom we were never allowed to hear about because he didn't believe in mixing his friends. There are some men and Sewell was one, whose company is sought because it is a supreme gift."

From *Robert My Father* by Sheridan Morley (Weidenfeld and Nicolson, 1993) p. 209.

Sewell was still very much part of our lives when Charlie and I first got together and their affection for each other was mutual. When Charlie and I married Sewell gave us two sets of beautiful silver teaspoons, one set was for now, he explained, a wedding gift and the other was for our silver wedding present, when he would no longer be around.

Godparents and religious education

Sherry was very lucky in his godparents. As well as Sewell there was Bully, Peter Bull, an incredibly funny character actor with a face and physique made to play Tenniel's Duchess in *Alice in Wonderland*. Bully had a formidable mother, Lady Bull, who had a lady's maid and companion called Jessie. When Peter was in *Waiting for Godot* at the Royal Court, Lady Bull and Jessie loyally came although Becket was not really their cup of tea. Afterwards Bully asked his mother what she had thought of the play. There was a pause and then Lady Bull said: "Jessie thought the orchestra rail was most beautifully polished."

The choice of godparents is always fraught with difficulties; do you choose those with children, those who have some sort of track record, or those without (those who have no divided loyalties but are an unknown quantity where (god) parenting is concerned)? Do you choose them for their wealth, hoping a bit will eventually come the godchild's way or for their sweetness of nature? Do you choose them for their moral guidance? And how do you know who will be in for the long haul, as it were? Will you still be friends with them 12 or 15 years on?

I was thrilled to be asked to be Daniel Chatto's godmother at 11 years of age and Daniel in turn became our daughter Daisy's godfather. Our son Jack got as godparents our friends Vivie Ross, a Quaker and Tony Longaretti, of Italian Catholic background. When Jack was about four and we were on holiday in Tuscany we went to the island in Lake Trasimeno. Jack learnt to swim on that occasion because the lake bottom was so muddy and squelchy he kept lifting his feet up — suddenly we found he was doing the doggy paddle. He and Daisy were dispatched to explore the tiny island, Isola Bella, and came rushing back to where Charlie and I were having an aperitivo. They'd been in one of the many churches and Jack was full of what he'd seen: "Mum, mum — there's a man in there" gesturing back to the church and "he's like this", standing with arms stretched out in crucifixion mode "and they're doing horrible things to him!" Daisy then sauntered up, saying from the superior viewpoint of six and a half: "I've *told* him it's Baby Jesus but he just doesn't get it." "We'll get Uncle Tony and Auntie Vivie to explain it to you when we get home," was my solution.

Sherry, Will and I were brought up vaguely Church of England. At Hurst Lodge, when it was time for confirmation classes, I went to one class before deciding attending any more would be a bore. I told the vicar I would not be returning. He enquired why and off the top of my head I said, a little wistfully, that I was afraid his god was not my god. As they say, there was no answer to that. When

Charlie and I were going to get married I went to see John Ratings, the Wargrave vicar and explained that I hadn't been confirmed. John enquired what star sign I was (Gemini) and what about Charlie? When I replied that he was an Aquarian, John beamed. "That's all right then," he said.

Peter Bull would usually come down to see us, just for the day on a Sunday. Bully was gay like Sewell but unlike Sewell who was solitary, Bully had an American boyfriend called Don. For some years Bully and Don ran an astrological shop in Kensington Church Street where they sold all manner of things. Don liked to guess, usually correctly, what star sign a customer was by the way they walked into the shop and surveyed the merchandise.

The importance of being Mr Mac

A memorable guest was Michael MacLiammoir, but alas only for one weekend. Michael, with his partner Hilton Edwards had founded the Gate Theatre in Dublin and given Orson Welles his first acting jobs.

Our local theatre was at Windsor and was run by John Counsell and his wife and daughters, all of whom acted in the productions. I so longed to be Elizabeth Counsell, strutting about in tights and boots as Dick Whittington in the Christmas panto. When the theatre was in financial difficulties Robert came up with a fairly painless way of raising money. There would be a charity benefit and anyone who had a one man show would come and do a bit of it. G was the slightly distrait Mistress of Ceremonies.

Michael MacLiammoir not only did a bit of his wonderful Oscar Wilde show but stayed with us for the weekend. We couldn't accommodate his boyfriend (not Hilton by then but a much younger chap) because of lack of space so he stayed in the pub in Wargrave.

However, he did arrive on the Saturday morning dressed in jodhpurs, boots and a tweed jacket. It seemed he had no intention of going near a horse, that's just what he wore in the country. Michael came down to breakfast on the Saturday morning in full make up, his blacker-than-a-raven's-wing toupee firmly glued down but slightly off centre, wearing a silk dressing gown and a cravat over his corset. My slightly stressed mother was heard telling Will he was to be a bit tidier than usual and think of others. "I haven't got time to be picking up after you", she said "what with the house full and Michael's make up all over the bathroom."

After the performance we sat round the kitchen table and Michael told us ghost stories; he was more Irish than the Irish because he was in fact born Alfred Willmore in Kensal Green and had been a child actor with Noël Coward. The Irish accent, the name were all wonderful inventions. "Spell binding" people sometimes say, too lightly about performers, but Mr Mac was a spell binder. He must have entranced Joan, I can't imagine her letting anyone else keep us all sitting around the kitchen table at midnight.

Colcannon is an Irish dish. It is simply equal quantities of potatoes and cabbage, which sounds boring but it is better than either ingredient on its own and a very good addition to a leg of slow cooked lamb.

Colcannon

4–6 large potatoes, peeled and cut up
½ a large Savoy cabbage, finely shredded
3–4 spring onions, chopped
50g butter
2–3 tbsp milk
salt and pepper

Mash the cooked potatoes with plenty of butter and some milk, salt and pepper. Cook the cabbage in a little water and drain well and mix the cabbage with the potatoes. Add the finely chopped spring onions, salt and pepper.

An estate agent, who called when the house was to be sold, sat at the dining room table and remarked on how many famous people must have sat there. The truth was that my parents never gave dinner parties; supper was usually eaten in front of the TV, everyone with their own little "occasional" table. In later years Joan cooked supper — often something from the supermarket if it was just her and Robert. If they had guests, she would push the boat out with a duck or trout, one of her specialities.

Robert used to say "there's nothing on a duck" and you are lucky to feed four from a duck. However, he also claimed roast potatoes cooked in duck fat were the best. Joan's ducks were always served with roast potatoes and green peas. I personally like the combination of either orange or cherries with duck.

Duck with oranges or cherries

Duck breasts are a good, easy way to serve duck, because there are no struggles with carving. Cook them following the instructions on the packet; I like duck well cooked, not pink. Remember to rest it after roasting so it's not rubbery. For the gravy leave a little fat in the pan, thicken with flour as if making a gravy, add some red wine and stock and either a segmented, peeled orange and a good tablespoon of orange marmalade or cherry jam, lemon juice and some dried cherries previously soaked in red wine. Peas and mashed potato are good with duck as is a watercress and chicory salad. If you do cook a whole duck, roast it for an hour to an hour and a half. To serve simply cut it in four with shears.

The first Christmas after Sewell died, Robert wrote:

> *"This year for the first time we have Christmas without him and I can't decide what to do: to put his present under the tree, open in vain his bedroom door and look for his Gladstone bag, for he never really totally unpacked? Better just perhaps to write about him this Christmas Eve and put away the letter along with the will and the birth certificate for others to read one day, particularly my elder son who was also his godson and so loved him as did we all who just now miss him so very much."*

From *Robert My Father* by Sheridan Morley (Weidenfeld and Nicolson, 1993) p. 210.

ROBERT AND SEWELL STOKES THE "AMI DU MAISON"
WE ALL LOVED

Outcast of the Islands (1952)

Chapter Seven

YOU OUGHTA BE IN PICTURES

I WAS FOUR when my father asked me if I wanted to be in a film. My answer was yes, as long as I could have plaits. My lack of hair (at four I only had a few white blonde curls) contributes to my earliest memory; in Central Park, New York a man peered into my pushchair and remarked what a cute little boy I was. My fine blonde babyish curls were a great disappointment to me, as I wanted to look like a friend of my elder brother's, Mary Anne Bellord, who had two long thick dark plaits.

The film was *Outcast of the Islands* from the novel by Joseph Conrad. In 1948 the producer Alexander Korda announced he was to make a film of Joseph Conrad's novel that would star Robert Mitchum as the anti-hero, Willems. Korda involved the director Carol Reed in the project in the early 1950s, wanting to follow up on the enormous success of *The Third Man*.

Alexander Korda was the Hungarian born movie mogul who had almost single-handedly created the British film industry. Carol Reed was the illegitimate son of the great actor manager Sir Herbert

Beerbohm Tree, who had failed to give Carol his distinguished name. Michael Korda, Alex's nephew, wrote in *Charmed Lives* of the relationship between Alex and Carol Reed and said that although Reed undoubtedly saw Korda as something of a father figure, it was difficult to say which one of them had adopted the other. Korda came to genuinely love Reed and took a kind of fatherly pride in his success. Michael wrote that "they brought out the best in each other."

Reed insisted on having Trevor Howard in the lead part, supposedly saying that he could think of no contemporary film actor better suited to play Willems, the moral degenerate, than Trevor. Conrad's novel, written in 1894, was set in Borneo, and was a prequel to his first novel, *Almayer's Folly*. The main characters are Lingard, a sea captain, Lingard's son-in-law a Dutch trader, Almayer and the outcast of the title, Willems, a swindler and wastrel. Willems is rescued from a scandal by Lingard and taken to his private fiefdom, a remote trading settlement, up an almost inaccessible and secret river. Lingard leaves Willems in the care of Almayer and his wife. The two men have a mutual dislike and contempt for each other. Willems is overwhelmed by his isolation and falls violently in love with a native woman, the daughter of the local chief. In thrall to her he reveals the secret passage up the river to Lingard's rivals, the Arab traders, and for this betrayal is exiled on a remote island with a bitter and vengeful Aissa. Conrad wrote that he had seen for himself what he called "…a fall, a sudden descent into physical enslavement by an absolutely untamed woman."

One of the problems with Conrad's novel was that there are no likable characters in the pessimistic story; the notices praised Reed's dogged skill in documenting Willem's decline into complete depravity and noted that the film bristled with tension. It looked good, designed by Korda's brother Vincent. Much of it was shot in Sri Lanka, where Reed found an enchanting local child who features in many of the establishing shots of native village. Location shooting was not without its problems, a second entire native village on stilts had to be built after the first one was washed away. Reed sprained his ankle and had to be carried up and down hills searching for camera set ups. After being unable to sleep because of the barking of the local dogs, Reed complained and then was horrified to find over a hundred of them had been shot.

Ralph Richardson, playing a generation older than his actual age in a lot of false whiskers, played Lingard. Ralph was married to the actress Meriel Forbes to whom my father had once tentatively proposed. I think of all his contemporaries Robert most admired Ralph as an actor. He was a very easy man to love. Carol Reed adored him and it was mutual, Ralph gave a magnificent reading at Carol's funeral. And Korda was one of Ralph's great patrons casting him again and again in his films.

Ralph was a perfectionist. On one particularly hot and steamy day on location for *Outcast* he was told that as he was only being shot in close up, so it wouldn't be necessary for him to be in full sea captain costume. However, he appeared correctly dressed down to the boots, explaining "If I wore my own shoes, it might show in the shot from the way I stood." A critic wrote of Ralph in *Outcast*, "Ralph Richardson at his best like a character from Ibsen, gives his lines a meaning and value beyond compare." (*What's On*, 8 January 1952.)

Ralph was famously eccentric. Well into his senior years he could be seen riding round London on his motor bike with Jose his pet parrot tucked inside his leather jacket. He also kept a ferret, Eddie, who he bathed weekly in Lux soap flakes. Acting, Ralph asserted once, is merely the art of keeping a large group of people from coughing. People admired Gielgud, adulated Olivier but were devoted to Richardson.

As the smouldering local beauty Korda cast a French Algerian girl he found selling jewellery in the South of France. Her name was changed from Miriam to Kerima. When she was considered to have an inadequate bosom, a special padded rubber bra was made for her which she found unbearable in the sultry heat. Miriam/Kerima is silent throughout the film, photographed often obliquely through the slats of the wooden walls, frequently having just had a bucket of water poured over her. After the location shooting the film was completed in England.

Wendy Hiller, who played Robert's wife and my mother, shared with her contemporaries Celia Johnson and Peggy Ashcroft a typically English temperament, charming, honest, frank and open without tricks or affectations in her performance. She was an acclaimed stage actress and her big break had come playing Sallie Hardcastle in *Love on the Dole* in 1935. During the Second World War she played Princess Charlotte, daughter to Robert's "Prinny", the Prince Regent (for his mad father George III) who became George IV. In the play *The First Gentleman* Robert told me that when they acted together:

> *"She was never afraid of overacting when she felt instinctively the role required her to do so. As Princess Charlotte she was in turn so fierce and so gentle, that on some evenings after she had died in the second act, it seemed a waste of time continuing with the play."*

Robert and Wendy played father and daughter again in the film of Shaw's *Major Barbara* in 1941. Wendy had had a great personal triumph as Eliza Doolittle in *Pygmalion* opposite Leslie Howard in 1938 — she lost out on an Oscar for that performance to Bette Davis. Wendy was married to a delightful man Ronald Gow, who had been a schoolmaster but who had adapted *Love on the Dole* for the stage. He and Wendy had two children, roughly contemporary with Sheridan and me, and we knew them well. Wendy gives the most subtle and moving portrayal in *Outcast*.

It was Wendy's first experience of working with Ralph Richardson and she remembered:

"When we were doing Outcast *the makeup room was upstairs and if I was coming downstairs and Ralph was going up I could see Ralph making up his mind who he was for that greeting — whether he was going to be hail-fellow-well-met or whether he was going to be very distant or whether he was going to put his arm around me or was he going to speak at all? I wasn't only unsure, he was unsure too and I think that was because he was so shy, he couldn't be himself, which was a very special and original self."*

From *Ralph Richardson: The authorized biography* by John Miller (Sidgwick and Jackson, an imprint of Macmillian General Books, 1995) p. 146.

For my father Robert it was his eleventh film; his film career had started in Hollywood in 1938 when he was cast as the doomed Louis XVI opposite Norma Shearer's *Marie Antoinette*.

"When Annabel and I made the film Outcast of the Islands, *she was only four at the time so my daughter did not arrive at the studio until comparatively late in the morning and slept for an hour after luncheon. Because of this and the immense care and patience with which Carol Reed directed it, the film took a considerable time to complete. There has never been a director with better manners or who shows more consideration for his cast."*

From *Robert Morley: Responsible Gentleman* by Robert Morley and Sewell Stokes (Heinemann, 1966) p. 171.

What do I remember of making the film? As my mother kept scrap books for us all, I know in January 1951 I went for the first time to Shepperton Studios with my parents and Nancy, my nanny. There I was fitted for the dress and plaits, great long plaits fixed to my head with Kirby grips and bows. We had lunch with Wendy Hiller.

The next day I went with my mother as Robert was already at the studios. I was made up, did some shots, spoke some lines and met the monkey who appears in one shot with me.

On 25 January we shot the scene where I greet Ralph Richardson, crying and reluctant to kiss him because as I protest "…his beard prickles me."

In early February we shot a scene which wasn't in the finished picture but involved Robert carrying me and running along several mattresses on rope bases. It was supposed to look as if were running across rice paddies, escaping from a water buffalo. I was wearing just a sarong and I remember Robert's shirt buttons digging in as he clutched me to him.

I also remember shooting the scene where Ralph Richardson builds me a house of cards; the cards were stuck together, which I thought a bit of a cheat. Because I had a lisp I couldn't say "Singapore" without it coming out as "Fingerpore" so there were many takes for that scene. As Robert remembered:

"I watched for two days while Ralph Richardson built a house of cards, a monkey perched on his shoulder and Annabel on his knee repeating over and over again the line 'Build me a house Grandpapa, like the one we are going to live in, in Singapore.' Each time the monkey would jump down, or the cards fall down, or my four year old daughter break down — and the scene would be spoilt. But when victory was achieved it was Annabel who clapped her hands and smiled reassuringly at Carol, 'Perfect, perfect' she echoed, 'just once more darling!'"

I behaved badly one day, "was rather temperamental" as my mother put it. The set which was our house was built up on stilts and somehow I crawled under the house and refused to come out for the scene which was Almayer's birthday party. Trevor, Robert and Wendy were all in this scene and so were two servants. I kept everybody waiting. Finally a small man, who was an electrician or "grip", crawled in and dragged me out but not before I bit him on the hand.

The scene most people remember was the one in which I am encouraged to call "Pig, pig, pig" as Trevor runs from the house. Having gone to live with Aissa, Willems returns to try and do a deal with Almayer over trading rights, only to be humiliated by him. The charming William Fairchild who wrote the screenplay, meeting me in Sydney in the late 1980s, said that he had written in more lines for me when he realised as he put it "you could do it."

The film received good notices, a typical one for Robert was:

"Robert Morley is excellent as the pompous schemer Almayer and a word of praise should be added for the delightful child who plays his daughter looking so like him I was not surprised to find she is Annabel Morley. Miss Morley is at the age when acting obviously comes naturally. I hope she can escape the self consciousness or self esteem which seems to attack most child actors. At the moment she shows rare promise."
(Clair Leng's Film Column, *Musical Express*, 25 January 1952)

Another notice said:

"For a delightful father and daughter team this film is a triumph. Robert Morley's brilliant performance as a neurotic trader is given delicious support by the prattlings of five year old Annabel, his real life daughter, this button nosed poppet is certainly an interesting discovery."
(*Halifax Weekly Courier*, 16 February 1952)

"A word of praise for Annabel Morley, even her father cannot prevent her from stealing almost every scene in which she appears."
(Margaret Constable, *Yorkshire Herald*, 25 January 1952)

"Next to animals the English love child actors. Five year old Annabel Morley of Outcast of the Islands *is the girl for my money, no retirement ahead for a lady of her block busting temperament."*
(Spotlight, *Vogue London*, April 1952)

Carol gave the credit for directing my performance to Robert: "I just told Mr Morley what I wanted to do and he took her away in a corner and practised it with her."
(*Daily Mail*, London, 16 January 1952)

Despite the notices it was never a popular success as a film, probably because there isn't a single likeable character.

Here is the only Sri Lankan recipe I know. We had it one New Year's Eve, it is delicate and rich, sweet and spicy.

Thakkali or prawn and tomato curry
(adapted from *Tamasin's Kitchen Classics* by Tamasin Day-Lewis [Weidenfeld & Nicolson, 2006])

675g green prawns in their shells
1 litre water
1 tbs vegetable oil
1 small red onion, finely chopped
a handful of curry leaves
2 tsp fenugreek
6 cloves of garlic, crushed
2 green chillies, seeded and finely chopped
1 tsp each roasted and ground cumin and coriander

2 tsp chilli powder
400g tin tomatoes
2–3 tbsp coconut cream
splash of fish sauce
juice of 1 lime

Shell the prawns and make a stock with the prawn shells and 1 litre of cold water, brought to the boil and simmered for 40 minutes. Strain and reserve the stock. Heat the oil in a heavy pan and add onion, curry leaves and fenugreek. Fry until lightly browned. Add garlic and chillies and then ground spices and chilli powder and fry gently, then add the prawn stock and reduce by half. Add tomatoes, coconut cream and fish sauce, stir and simmer uncovered until the sauce is thick. Lastly add the prawns and cook gently until they become pink and opaque, add lime juice to taste.

SERVES 4

There is a post script to *Outcast*. Bizarrely it was chosen for the Royal Command Film Performance of 1953 and Robin Fox, Robert's agent rang Korda to congratulate him. "But" said Robin, "there is the matter of my client's outstanding fee." "Nonsense", said Korda, "Robert has been paid." "Not Robert," said Robin, "but my client Miss Annabel Morely. She has never had a contract and no fee was paid." Korda pointed out that I was a child — even so, Robin insisted I should be paid. "There is a Pissarro landscape in the window of Browse and Delbanco," said Korda, who knew a thing or two about pictures. "I will pay half what they are asking for it and Robert should pay half, it will be a good investment."

So *Apple Orchard at Pontoise* hung in the sitting room to the right hand side of the fireplace for 20 years. Then Robert was selling something, the Utrillo. The man from Sotheby's told Robert it wasn't a particularly wonderful Utrillo, but on the other hand, that it was a nice little Pissarro and he hoped Robert had it insured for the correct amount. Upping the insurance alerted the insurance company to the fact that the house was not exactly burglar proof. The front door didn't even have a key and the backdoor was usually unlocked. Even a fairly incompetent burglar could have broken through the French windows that led from the garden. We had a family conference, I could see my parents didn't want to install burglar alarms or have security locks. The Pissarro would be sold. When we delivered it to Sotheby's, they placed it on a red velvet easel, beautifully lit. Robert and I gasped. Having previously only ever seen the picture in the sitting room at "Fairmans", with its low ceilings, white washed walls, where one was never further away than the width of the room from a painting, now it was as if we saw the picture for the first time, in all its beautiful, glowing autumnal colour. The auction itself was thrilling and a Swiss man bought "my" Pissarro. I have never seen it in an exhibition but then I've never tried to trace it.

"Build me a house, Grandpapa, like the one we're going to live in, in Europe." Ralph Richardson and Abbie, *Outcast of the Islands* (1952)

Robert, Joan and Will in Venice (1956)

Chapter Eight

MAKING A SCENE

Italy

In 1952 Sheridan and I, without my younger brother Wilton, who was only a baby, went with my parents to Italy, to Ravello where Robert was filming, *Beat the Devil*. It had taken me some years to realise that, unlike other little girls' fathers who went off on the Paddington train to make money in banks and offices, mine pretended, not always convincingly, to be someone else for his living. One of the perks of being Robert's child was joining him on location. My mother told me we would be staying with a prince in Italy. The only prince I could visualise was the one in the Walt Disney version of *Cinderella* so when we got to Ravello, on the Amalfi coast of Italy and I was introduced to Prince Tasca, he was something of a disappointment. He was small middle aged man in a grey suit. He did however bend low over my mother's hand and kiss it.

Beat the Devil was directed by John Huston who also wrote the script with Truman Capote. The cast included Humphrey Bogart,

Jennifer Jones and Gina Lollobrigida (known to the cast and crew as La Frigidaire). A fairly incomprehensible story was made even harder to follow by the fact that Huston and Capote wrote the scenes as they went along. Then Tru suddenly couldn't write any more. It seemed his pet raven in Rome was sulking in his absence and refused to speak to him on the phone. This, not unnaturally, depressed him and he and Huston hit the bottle to an even greater extent than was usual for them. This lack of clarity and direction was not just confusing, but also dangerous. One scene involved a car being sent over a cliff, supposedly with Bogart inside. The plan was that he would appear to be driving while a small Italian mechanic crouched on the floor, operating the pedals. At a given signal he and Bogart would leap out of the car, just before it ran over the cliff. There was no signal given but Bogart looked down as the car gathered speed and realised the mechanic had jumped ship as it were, so he threw himself out just in time. "John," he said rather mildly to Huston, "I could have been killed."

Jennifer Jones, who was fairly dotty, took a fancy to me and indulged me in my passion for being read to. On one memorable occasion my mother, looking for me, heard Jennifer's voice reading a story, opened the door but couldn't see anyone in the room. Jennifer and I, for some unknown reason, were perched on top of a large armoire.

On the way to Ravello we went to Rome where I lay down on the floor in the middle of St Peter's and complained that everything was "too big". My father, endlessly indulgent, carried me out, saying "You are absolutely right."

During filming Robert wrote progress reports on the filming to his mother.

February 23 1953, Villa Sangro, Ravello (before we joined him in Italy) from letters to his mother: "We are here at last and very *comfortable in a villa rented by the film company from some Duke and in which the King stayed when he abdicated. Sharing the villa is Prince Tasca who is in charge of the location arrangements. It is all very en prince naturally, with a good many servants fetching and carrying. The villa has the most lovely views over the sea and a terrace where we lunch and lie in the sun. We have a very glamorous cast what with Bogart, Jennifer Jones and Lola Brigida (Gina Lollobrigida) who is Italy's top star so the villagers are thrilled and wait to cheer Miss Brigida whenever she leaves the hotel.*

Apparently they expect to spend all of a hundred thousand pounds in Italy alone. This may be the last of these extravagant pictures but then I always think that and they seem to go on."

March 9: "Well, here we all are. I went up to Rome on Saturday and met Joanie and Sherry and Abbie who arrived on the comet. We took the children on a helter skelter tour of the sights on Sunday morning. Abbie thought the churches too big, which they are, and Sherry, who hates sightseeing anyway, was only really interested by a model flying club display which we happened to pass. However I've done my best to give them culture.

The film progresses by fits and starts, mostly the former. We haven't really got a script, which makes things harder than they need be. The children are perfectly happy as long as they are buying endless and useless souvenirs and nothing is too hideous or expensive not to be immediately coveted. You ask what the film is called and what my part is about... all I know is it's called Beat the Devil *and I think I play a crook. I am being paid just the ten thousand pounds to keep my mouth shut and when it's finished plan to take the rest of the year off to write a book and a play."*

(Undated): "It's really hot again and we go down to beaches and Abbie actually bathed or at any rate sat in the sea although the water

seemed very cold to me. The film goes slowly and I should think another month will see us heading for home. It will I fear be a very bad film as the story, which gets rewritten every evening, seems to grow more feeble and makeshift. They (the cast and crew) are all very nice and the villa is a dream of comfort and the most wonderful food, everyone else who are not doing so well in the local hotels tries to move in with us but so far we have managed to beat off all invaders. Sherry amuses himself taking everyone's photo and Abbie chums up with Jennifer Jones who buys her chocolate ice creams and thoroughly spoils her."

March 31 (we had gone home by now): "I have spent the last two days cruising along the coast in a tramp steamer making the film which continues fairly smoothly. We had two nights shooting round the docks past Salerno which was boring and surprisingly cold.

We have been filming in a monastery which is a boys' school and very uncomfortable and depressing. I am glad Sherry doesn't have to go to school in Italy, he'd hate it.

The children were very sweet and good out here and Abbie actually ate quite a lot or at least more than she does at home. I think she'll rather miss the meat which is very good here. They liked the beaches best and Positano beach best of all, it's a sweet little place with a charming little restaurant on the sands. The people although very poor prefer to earn their money day to day carrying loads on their heads rather than take regular employment in factories or as servants."

April 10: "We have a lot of visitors who come and go. The latest have been George Saunders and Ingrid Bergman who were filming further along the coast and used to come up to Ravello in the evening. George brought his wife who is by way of being a film star and very exotic (Zsa Zsa Gabor) to dinner in the villa and made me laugh a good deal about their life together in Hollywood where the columnists keep writing that they are separated and no one believes it except Mrs

Saunders who doesn't really trust George much."

May 12 (from home): "Jolly glad to be back although I enjoyed Italy except the last day or two when we were stuck in a miserable little place called Sabaudia about 80 miles from Rome on the Pontine Marshes. It poured with rain for three days and I thought we would never get the scenes taken and get home but miraculously it cleared up on Friday morning and we finished two days' work in three hours which only shows what they can do if they try. I spent a night in Naples en route for Sabaudia, we were very gay and went to a night club and I had half a bottle of champagne (about) and felt simply terrible the next day. I can't drink it any more I fear."

Austria

I was 11 and Will 6, when Robert made a film in Vienna. *The Journey* was about a group of travellers caught up in the Hungarian Uprising. Yul Brynner played a Russian army officer. Robert wrote in a letter to Joan at the beginning of the shoot:

"Yul Brynner seems rather pleasant although very short…he calmly announced at lunch that he thought of having his tonsils out tomorrow which would delay us a good deal although he isn't in at the beginning of the film…he plays a Russian and makes his first appearance on a black stallion but as he seems to have put up most of the money for the picture I guess he's entitled to it."

Deborah Kerr and Jason Robards were the romantic leads.
There were two little American boys in the film, one of them Ron Howard. They played the sons of Anne Jackson, who was heavily pregnant both in the film and in real life and her husband

Eli Wallach flew out to give comfort and support — which was how my parents met the Wallachs, who became great friends.

When we went out to stay with Robert on the location we joined him in the incredibly grand Hotel Imperial. It had been quite recently refurbished after the wartime damage caused by the Russians who had stabled their horses in the dining room. In Robert's opinion the best thing about the hotel was the staff who were "terribly good and the food and the plumbing also very superior." Will and I had a game we played at meal times, which was to see how many times we could accidentally-on-purpose drop our table napkins, which would then be whisked away by a waiter and a fresh one laid on our laps.

We also went to that wonderful fun fair, the one that features in *The Third Man*, and came back with helium balloons, which immediately floated out of our reach up to the high ceilings of our bedrooms. Hotel staff arrived with stepladders to recapture the balloons.

I clearly remember a beautiful restaurant in the countryside with a pool of trout, several of which ended up fried and succulent on our plates for lunch. Perhaps we had that sublime Austrian chocolate cake, Sachertorte.

Sachertorte

    375g dark chocolate
    250g butter
    200g castor sugar
    5 large eggs, separated
    1½ tbsp self raising flour
    80g ground almonds
    3 heaped tbsp apricot jam

Melt 250g of the chocolate. Cream 125g of the butter with the castor sugar and beat in the chocolate. Beat in egg yolks, one at a time. Whisk the egg whites stiffly. Fold in the egg whites alternately with the sifted flour mixed with the ground almonds. Bake in a greased, lined 20cm cake tin at 180°C for 45 minutes or until a skewer comes out clean. When cool, cut in half, spread bottom half with apricot jam and then sandwich back together.

Melt remaining butter and chocolate to make a ganache, cool in the refrigerator until set enough to use to ice the cake.

SERVES 8–10

France

Robert worked on the movie *Topkapi* in Paris in the winter of 1964. Most of Jules Dassin's film had been shot in Istanbul. I particularly remember watching on the set for a bedroom scene between Melina Mercouri (married to Dassin) and Maximillian Schell. I was fascinated by Melina, her rather badly dyed blonde hair, deep husky voice and particularly the way she painted over her toe nail varnish with another colour, deep green, without removing the old polish. Dassin or Julie as everyone called him, adored her.

In the mid-sixties Robert made a film called *Hotel Paradiso* also in Paris. He took me to Nancy Mitford's elegant abode on the Rue Monsieur where she entertained us and Lesley Blanch, a neighbour, dropped in. These two unbelievably elegant women suggested Robert take me to one of the great couture houses to see a collection. Nancy wrote of Robert: "…nobody makes me laugh like him, and although wicked to work with, in private life a sort of angel." She described me as "Robert's fat sweet daughter." (Charlotte Mosely (ed), *The Mitfords: Letters between Six Sisters* [Harper, 2007] p. 440)

Robert never had a very high opinion of the French. He wrote in a letter to his mother:

> *"I don't like the French, they seem to take such ages choosing their food and lovers and so little time enjoying them, in fact I don't think I've ever seen a Frenchman look as if he was enjoying anything."*

Robert took me to a restaurant in Paris where they only served pâtés and terrines and puddings, my idea of heaven.

Chicken, pork and veal terrine with cherry sauce

pancetta or bacon to line 1.5 litre terrine or tin
1 tbs olive oil
1 small onion finely chopped
1 garlic clove crushed
2 tsp chopped thyme leaves
750g pork and veal mince
1 egg, lightly beaten
½ cup fresh breadcrumbs
½ cup pistachio kernels
1 cup (150g) pitted cherries
3 chicken tenderloin fillets, trimmed

CHERRY SAUCE

1 cup pitted cherries
100g dried cranberries
finely grated zest and juice of 1 orange
1 cinnamon quill
⅓ cup (75g) caster sugar
¼ cup marsala

Preheat oven to 170°C.

Line terrine or tin with pancetta or bacon slices. Leave enough to cover the top of the terrine. Heat oil in a frying pan and fry the onion, garlic and thyme until the onion is soft. Cool slightly and then process with mince, egg, breadcrumbs. Season with salt and pepper. Stir in pistachios and cherries. Put half the mixture in the terrine and arrange chicken down the centre, cover with the rest of the mixture and press down. Cover with remaining pancetta or bacon. Cover with foil and place in a roasting tin. Fill roasting tin with enough boiling water to come half way up the terrine. Bake for an hour. Remove from oven and place on tray. Weigh down with cans or weights and chill overnight.

For sauce: Place all ingredients in a saucepan and stir over medium heat to dissolve sugar. Cook, stirring occasionally for 15 minutes. Cool. Serve with terrine.

SERVES 6–8

Spain

In 1969 we were in Spain, in the Basque country, near Pamplona where Robert filmed *Cromwell*. Alec Guinness played Charles I and Richard Harris, Cromwell. There were lots of lovely young men playing Cavaliers and Roundheads, the Spanish army playing both. It was a strange location, a plain with a microclimate all its own which stood in for all the battlefields. The cast and crew spent a lot of time sitting around in tents, playing cards and eating the excellent location grub. A huge plus as far as I was concerned was the presence of Charles Gray, a wonderfully urbane and amusing actor. I started drinking Negronis, CG's favourite tipple, in an effort to be sophisticated. One night a few of us went to a bar, including Charles, and I asked one of the young actors I was particularly friendly with, if he thought it was remotely possible CG fancied me as he was being very, very nice to me and I had developed a huge crush on him. Kindly, my new friend said he didn't really think so, particularly as CG had just asked the waiter for his phone number.

After the location Robert and I went to Madrid, to the Prado and to Toledo, sinister and darkly glittering, with that curiously repellent bloodthirsty Catholicism informing everything.

I can't say I'm mad about Spanish food but I love gazpacho.

Gazpacho

(adapted from *At Elizabeth David's Table*, compiled by Jill Norman [Michael Joseph, 2010] p. 48.)

> 500g raw, peeled tomatoes
> 500g peeled tomatoes
> ¼ telegraph cucumber, diced
> 2 cloves garlic, chopped
> 1 spring onion
> 12 stoned black olives
> 3 tbsp olive oil
> 1 tbs red wine vinegar
> salt and pepper
> a little chopped marjoram, mint or parsley

Chop tomatoes until they are almost a puree. Stir in cucumber, garlic, finely sliced spring onion, olives, olive oil, red wine vinegar, salt, pepper, marjoram, mint or parsley.

Serve very cold with ice cubes in the bowls.

Miss David adds strips of green pepper to her soup but I am allergic to peppers so I put little bowls of strips of peppers on the table for guests to add to the soup. More diced cucumber and chopped hard boiled eggs are also good additions.

Hawaii

The last time I was with Robert on a location was in Hawaii in 1987, for an interminable made-for-TV-series: *War and Remembrance* in which Robert played a war correspondent.

It was not Robert's first visit to Hawaii because we and G had gone there on our world trip with *Edward My Son* in 1949. Then Robert described eating in a "native" restaurant in another letter to his mother:

> *"Hawaiian food is filthy, consisting of scraps of old pig and a sort of gloomy porridge into which everything else is dipped, preferably by hand."*

In *War and Remembrance* Robert had to play a death scene, on board a destroyer during the battle of the Coral Sea. He liked to knock off clothes from films and had his eye on the tropical-weight cream linen suit he was wearing on set. A fellow actor, Ian McShane, confided to me that he was worried about Robert having to fall down on the deck of the ship. I said I was sure Robert would be very careful of himself, and particularly the suit.

I didn't go out to the ship for the filming since once there out on the ocean there was no way of getting back until the end of the day. Plus the one ship, which had one side painted as an American destroyer and other side painted as a Japanese war ship, was surrounded by the smoke used to simulate battle conditions, created by burning smelly rubber tyres.

Robert and I had a routine which was for me to collect him

from his room in the hotel at the cocktail hour whereupon we would go and have a pre-dinner drink. As I approached his room on the evening on the death scene day, I could hear muffled swearing. Despite his best efforts there was blood on the beautiful cream coloured suit. "Bloody fool of a make-up man," said Robert, "look at it…blood all over the lapel." I rang the make-up department who assured me the theatrical blood was water-based. I put a note on the suit to that effect and sent it to be dry-cleaned. It came back clean and Robert wore the pristine suit for the few summers he had left. For the first time I became aware of his age (79) when on the beach at Waikiki I had to help him out of the sea, through the surf.

What can one say about American food? Hawaii of course is America, give or take a bit of Mahai Mahai. The plethora of ads on American TV for remedies for heartburn, "acid stomach" and indigestion speaks volumes. I find that the food itself has very little taste and is usually under-seasoned. The size of the portions and the convention of serving salad first — both these amaze me.

The following recipe isn't, strictly speaking, an American one but I made this pie for a Thanksgiving dinner and pecans I feel are very American. If you can find Carème brand ready-made pastry, buy the chocolate one for this.

Chocolate and pecan pie

>   250g short crust pastry, chocolate if possible
>   75g plain dark chocolate, finely chopped
>   75g butter
>   2 medium eggs
>   75g castor sugar
>   200g golden syrup
>   1 tsp vanilla extract

100g pecans, finely chopped plus 100g whole pecan halves to decorate

Preheat oven to 180°C. Put a baking sheet in the oven to heat up. Roll out pastry and use to line a 20.5 x 3cm loose-bottomed tin (a quiche tin is good). Chill until needed. Melt chocolate and butter in a heatproof bowl over simmering water and cool slightly. In a large bowl beat together eggs, sugar, golden syrup, vanilla and cooled chocolate mixture. Fold in chopped pecans, then pour into pastry case and decorate with whole pecans. Put pie on hot baking sheet in oven and bake 40–45 minutes until just set. Serve warm or at room temperature with cream or vanilla ice cream.

SERVES 8

Family holidays

Early family holidays were usually spent on some windswept English beach, West Wittering or the Isle of Wight. However, at some point Robert must have had enough of those because after *Beat the Devil* we started to go to the Lido in Venice.

We stayed at the Hotel de Bains, walked down to our allotted cabana on the beach, and swam and played on the immaculate sand, raked every morning by men in straw hats and faded red cotton shirts. Hotel guests had their own cabanas, with blue and white striped day beds on which the day's supply of clean towels was folded. The hotel had an extension of its restaurant on the beach and we would wander up the sand for lunch. When asked what we wanted to eat, Will and I would answer carrots, knowing perfectly well that when my mother enquired after their availability the waiter would sigh sadly and reply that alas, there were none. "A little green salad or a bean or two?" The bambini were insistent and consistent in their demand for carrots. One day the waiter came down to the beach to meet us, his face wreathed in smiles "Signora," he said triumphantly to my mother, "today, we 'ave carrots!" As if we had rehearsed our response, both Will and I said firmly that we didn't want carrots today. Why the waiter and/or my mother didn't kill us I don't know.

Will's birthday was in August so he would often have his birthday on the Lido. For his fourth birthday my mother invited a few other small children to a party. She thought it polite to forewarn the people in the next cabana, Lord Thorneycroft, Chairman of the Conservative Party and his elegant Italian wife, Carla, that there would be some small children bursting balloons and eating birthday cake. The Thorneycrofts it turned out were also having guests for tea, the Duke and Duchess of Windsor. The parties amicably mixed but my mother got stuck entertaining the Duke of Windsor who she described as a nice but dull little man.

In memory of those first English beach holidays when we went shrimping, here is a version of something my big brother loved, potted shrimps. These were manufactured by a firm called Young's and they came in waxed blue cardboard containers. Tiny, pinkish brown shrimps under a layer of clarified butter with a hint of something spicy, cayenne pepper? We used to spread them on hot toast.

Potted prawns

> 125g unsalted butter, melted and cooled
> 4 spring onions, chopped
> ½ cup mayonnaise (I like to use Paul Newman's Aioli or Hellman's mayo)
> 2 tbs lemon juice

2 tsp horseradish
1 tablespoon chopped parsley
¼ teaspoon cayenne, salt and pepper to taste
500g of cooked prawns, peeled to give 300g

In a food processor, combine butter, spring onions, mayonnaise, lemon juice, horseradish, parsley and seasonings with half the prawns. Don't over process, you want a textured end product. Add the rest of the prawns, whole or cut in half if very large. Put in little ramekins or one dish and pour over some more melted butter, decorate with sprigs of dill. Serve with hot toast.

SERVES 4

ABBIE, SHERRY AND WILL ON A FAMILY HOLIDAY (1954)

Abbie and Robert dressing up during the run of
The Little Hut (1952)

Chapter Nine

THE PLAY'S THE THING

In 1952 Robert was back in the West End with a play called *The Little Hut*. The play had a very good pedigree, originally it was a rather risqué French farce by Andre Roussin, but was transformed into a West End comedy by Nancy Mitford, who was famously pro-French. The plot concerns a lover, a husband and a wife who are washed up on a desert island, still in the evening clothes they were wearing when the ship was wrecked. They must not only accommodate themselves to life on the island but work out a *modus vivandi* — hence the little hut as well as the big hut, so both men can share the attentions of the wife. The play was directed by Peter Brook, the wonder boy of the English theatre at that time. It was designed by Oliver Messell and the set was dominated by a palm tree. This was a whimsical, beautiful palm tree with reinforced fronds that could support Robert when he wanted to sit down and be climbed by William Chappell, the stage manager who doubled as a monkey.

On the tour of *The Little Hut*, Robert stopped off at Balmoral Castle — which was "hideous" in his opinion — for Nancy Mitford to sightsee. "I am v. fond of her, I must say" he wrote to his mother. "Nancy's father came to the play at Newcastle — very smart and eccentric — the Uncle Matthew of her books." Her father said he hadn't read her books, but a friend had and had told him they were inaccurate. "Poor Nancy doesn't know the difference between a hunting whip and a riding crop; and it's too late to tell her now."

The tour started in Edinburgh; at the dress rehearsal there was no sign of Nancy and after the first act, Robert rang her at her hotel, to find she'd gone to bed. He reminded her she was supposed to be at the theatre, watching them. "Good gracious," she said "You poor dears, are you doing it tonight? I thought you were doing it tomorrow." "We are doing it tomorrow" Robert replied. "That's all right then", said Nancy, "that's when I'll see it."

Joan Tetzel, a sharp-faced American beauty, played the wife and her dress was designed by Balmain, the great French couturier. The beautiful and expensive evening dress had to look as if, like its wearer, it had survived a ship wreck, but naturally the wardrobe mistress was nervous of doing too much damage to it. The great man himself came to a rehearsal, leapt up on stage, borrowed a pair of scissors and slashed and tore the creation. It was still a beautiful dress but now it looked convincingly like one that had survived seawater and been dragged up a sandy beach. Robert always remembered Monsieur Balmain and the scissors as a supreme example of confidence, of an expert knowing exactly what he was doing.

On the pre-London tour in Manchester, Robert was still trying to get the play right. There was a conference after the performance which went on in Robert's bedroom in the hotel. My mother had come to see the play and was not best pleased at being kept awake by the discussion over technicalities which was going on around her. At some point, her patience snapped, "I can see why you are having problems," she said to Peter Brook, "you call yourself a director but you don't seem able to even ensure the stage is swept properly. Robert is walking round all night in bare feet and when he comes to bed he makes the hotel sheets filthy." It was the proverbial last straw and Peter Brook burst into tears. Ever after, when there was an occasion on which my mother might have spoken sharply, someone would say: "Well, of course, she did make Peter Brook cry."

The Little Hut was the beginning of my father's great friendship with David Tomlinson who became a frequent visitor to "Fairmans". I apparently nearly wrecked his chances with Audrey, who became his wife. On first being introduced to her, I am told I screwed up my face and asked David, "What happened to the Fwench lady?" referring to a previous "squeeze" David had brought to tea in the garden.

Ten years younger than Robert, David was a perfect foil to him with his expert timing, his charm and his eccentricity. Robert loved acting with people who shared his philosophy, who didn't take themselves too seriously and who could be entertaining companions in the theatre, share in the success if it was available but not be too gloomy if business was bad. Robert usually had a percentage of the takings and so would anxiously listen through the tannoy in the dressing room to see what kind of and how large an audience were filing into their seats. Then, before the curtain rose — and there was always in those days a curtain to rise and fall — he would go on stage and peer through the curtains and count the house. He would write down an estimate of the number of patrons and a calculation of the takings and then check with the front of house manager when the box office receipts were in. His gambler's ability to calculate possible revenue was usually spot on.

Other aspects of finance left him cold. It was my mother Joan who kept the household accounts and Robert's agent, Robin Fox, who was charged with keeping tabs on his earnings. Robert's proud boast was that he had never filled in a cheque stub. Of course, he was the despair of accountants and he fought pitched battles with the Inland Revenue over back taxes. His trump card was always to threaten bankruptcy which ultimately had the effect of some kind of deal over payment being made, but it was usually a white knuckle ride. Luckily Joan's more sober attitude to money balanced Robert's more exuberant one. When he came home in despair and announced that he owed £20,000 in back taxes and we were, in effect, penniless, my mother seemed not to be paying much attention. When challenged, she said she had been listening but, she said, there was nothing much to be done about that, however he could ring the builders and tell them the tiles for the bathroom were quite the wrong colour. Grounded, I think you could say.

Music and culture

When my father said he tried to give us culture, he was of course, saying it ironically. There was no music in our house to speak of, no classical music that is. We had a gramophone and a set of South Pacific '78s. They were in an album with a photograph of Mary Martin and Enzio Pinza and a waving palm tree on the cover. Sherry had LPs: Noel Coward, Tom Lehrer, Edith Piaf and Juliette Greco but my mother never sang or hummed or whistled about the house. If you were around G, you heard a sort of little whistled tune as she moved from room to room. My nanny, Nancy Stubbs sang songs to me: *Dashing away with the smoothing iron; Soldier, soldier won't you marry me? Little brown jug how I love thee; My father was a Spanish captain.*

Robert was, by his own admission completely tone deaf. Amazingly, he was in a musical at the Theatre Royal in Drury Lane in 1956. *Fanny* was taken from the Maurice Pagnol novels, stories of the Marseilles waterfront. Robert played Panisse who falls in love with Fanny — who has been left pregnant by her young sailor lover, Marius. The first act curtain rose to reveal the waterfront, little restaurants and bars, plus a fish stall. The actor Michael Gough played a rather sinister sailor in a striped Breton jersey.

One night I was allowed to hide on stage in one of the little shops for the first musical number. As the curtain rose on the huge auditorium, and a smattering of audience (it was not a great success) I could see out through the gauze but couldn't be seen. An American actress called Janet Pavek played Fanny and I had a huge crush on her. I saved up my pocket money to buy her a present, soap. Then Robert crushingly told me that the only reason you gave someone soap was to imply they didn't wash enough and were a bit smelly.

We were sometimes taken to lunch in London at a restaurant called the Trocadero where there was a band. The best thing about the Trocadero was every child got a present. It was usually something very inexpensive like a colouring book or a small puzzle, always unisex and wrapped in lovely garish paper which ripped easily. When we went to lunch there during the run of *Fanny* the band would strike up Robert's number *Love is a very light thing* and we'd have to alert Robert to the fact that that was what they were playing so he could acknowledge the band leader with a gracious gesture as he sat down. It was odd that, although he sang the song every night and twice on Wednesdays and Saturdays, he never recognised the melody.

Robert loved being in *Fanny* and never cared how few people were in front as long as he could be on stage pretending to sing and dance for them. Ian Wallace, who was a real opera singer, played Panisse's friend Cesar and had a song about coming home and how a house welcomes you, in which one of the lyrics was "you're back where you belong" — exactly how we all felt about coming home to "Fairmans".

A Likely Tale

When Robert did a play called *A Likely Tale*, in which he played a dual role of father and son, just before the run of *Fanny* in 1956, Margaret Rutherford played his sister/daughter. Mentally fragile, she started unravelling during rehearsals. Partly because he was genuinely fond of her and partly out of self-interest — because he didn't want the production jeopardised — Robert asked Margaret to come and stay with us. Did they go on rehearsing? I rather think they did. She was exactly like she is in films, with a sort of childlike innocence and sense of fun. I had met her previously during the filming of *Murder at the Gallop*.

It was winter when she came to us, nearly Christmas, and at some point in her visit she produced the most beautiful Christmas decorations for the tree. There was a tiny basket with glass fruit in it, the grapes were minute black glass beads.

One thing that really worried my mother was that Margaret would set off for a walk in the late afternoon gloom. The narrow country roads were dangerous at the best of times for a solitary walker; Margaret strode out in her tweed cape, the very image of Miss Marple or Madame Arcati sans bicycle. She always returned safely but my mother would be glancing at the clock and listening for the sound of the back door opening. I remember there also had to be sandwiches for her in case she woke up in the night and needed sustenance. I was very envious of the crustless, chicken sandwiches my mother cut and put on a plate by Margaret's bedside. I don't think you can beat a good chicken sandwich. This is how I make mine.

Chicken sandwiches

white or brown bread
poached chicken, chopped or shredded (3–4 chicken breasts
will give you enough sandwiches for 6–8 people)
2–3 stalks celery
2 tbsp parsley
½ cup walnuts
3–4 tbsp mayonnaise

In a food processor, blitz celery, parsley and walnuts. Add to chicken with a generous amount of mayonnaise, Hellman's or S and W. Spread on bread. Season well with salt and pepper.

The sandwiches should be generously filled, crustless and cut in fingers.

SERVES 6–8

Thirty years ago, or thereabouts, my brother Wilton, then a theatrical producer, brought Lauren Bacall from America to star in Tennessee William's *Sweet Bird of Youth*. Miss Bacall, Betty to her friends, arrived in Sydney to rehearse the show. My brother was then renting a large and beautiful house in Wolseley Road which had a swimming pool. Miss Bacall would swim in the pool every Sunday morning; my brother had to vacate the house while she was doing this — was she swimming in the nude? After her swim she wanted chicken sandwiches and iced tea. This was before iced tea was commercially available but after a few attempts I managed something I thought would pass muster. Will would come over and collect a thermos and the chicken sandwiches while Betty did her lengths.

After the first night of *Sweet Bird* Will gave a lavish party on a boat on Sydney Harbour. He led me to the table where Betty was sitting:

"May I introduce my sister, Annabel? She has been making you the chicken sandwiches."

Betty looked up at me: "Too much mayo in the chicken sandwiches, honey. If you use butter, you don't need so much mayo."

And nice to meet you too, I said, but silently.

Since then, no one else has complained, and I continue to make my sandwiches with both butter and mayo. Lots of mayo.

How the Other Half Loves

A play that was the reason Robert and I spent almost six months together in 1972. *How The Other Half Loves* by Alan Ayckbourn was a comedy about three couples whose lives become complicated and entangled. The pivotal scene was two dinner parties, with the couple who had been asked to both, swivelling in their chairs as the scene's focus shifted from one disastrous dinner to the other. The grandest couple, Frank and Fiona served fricadelles of veal at their dinner.

Veal and pork fricadelles (veal and pork meatballs)

> 1 small onion, finely chopped
> 500g pork and veal mince, equal quantities of each
> a large handful of fresh breadcrumbs, soaked in a little milk and squeezed out
> 1 clove garlic, crushed
> salt and pepper
> 1 tin chopped tomatoes

Combine everything except the tomatoes in a food processor and then form mixture into small meatballs. Roll these in seasoned plain flour and fry in a large frying pan in a mixture of olive oil and butter. When the meatballs are browned all over, put in an overproof dish and pour over tomatoes. Season with salt, pepper and a little sugar. Add some fresh basil or dried oregano. Cook at 180°C for about half an hour and serve with pasta or rice.

Robert played Frank, but he played it as he wanted to, which was not necessarily how the part had been written. Ayckbourn's play was an ensemble piece; Robert turned it into a star vehicle. Worse than that, from Ayckbourn's point of view, was that Robert refused to play Frank as the pompous, rather unpleasant, upper middle class bully he was on the page. "My public come to see me, lovable, bumbling, a bit eccentric, that's how I'm playing Frank." Frank's wife Fiona was a bit of a bitch; Robert cast his old friend Joan Tetzel who had played the naughty wife in *The Little Hut* as Fiona, but she wasn't going to play nasty either. Ayckbourn was in despair. "I'm going to make you very unhappy, Mr Ayckbourn," Robert told him, "and very, very rich."

We took *How the Other Half Loves* to Australia. It was an extensive tour, taking in all the major cities except Brisbane. However, my mother didn't want to be away from home for such a long stint. So it was decided that if I went with Robert we could rent an apartment or a house and I could be his social secretary.

In January 1972, en route we stopped at Bangkok for four days. It was my first taste of the East, and I adored it. On the plane we were befriended by an English travel writer who asked if he could show us some of the sights of Bangkok 1973: the floating market, the Emerald Buddha, even some strip joints. The travel writer took me to dinner on a floating restaurant, a converted rice barge. Business wasn't exactly booming, we were the only diners, but gliding along the Chao Phraya River eating a succession of beautiful little dishes under a starry sky was memorably romantic.

From my diary:

"Up the river in the morning to go to the floating markets, the first thing is rust-coated barges each with its crew of four or five having breakfast. People live on, in and off the river. Transport from house to house is by a boat, raised at one end, at one time brightly painted now faded and cracked. There are floating shops, greengrocers, a wonderful old fashioned haberdasher and draper, something one might see in Rye, teak and glass cases filled with salmon pink whalebone corsets, presided over by two old grandmas. A man cleaned his teeth and spat the Pepsodent a foot from my face, mothers held their babies out to crap in the river. Girls washed themselves and their clothes, neatly wrapped in sarongs — beautiful bodies and faces. Smiling, everyone smiles all the time, children on the river bank grin and mimic sunglasses and cameras, sending up the tourists and swim right up to the boat. The children swim in their clothes. Everyone's clothes on dry land look fresh-pressed and very clean. The houses are ramshackle, corrugated iron and bamboo or grander teak panelled or painted like Russian houses. The gardens are pots of purple orchids. Many people have dogs, walking nimbly on the landing stages or on teak logs."

Bruised frangipani blossoms were sold by little boys at street corners. We also saw novice monks being initiated in the Marble Wat and drinking Coca Cola. There was the awful squalor of Wat Arun, the Temple of Dawn made of pieces of broken ceramics and with scaffolding round it. That same Wat seen from the floating restaurant in the thin moonlight was a place of still beauty.

Thailand was a place of contrasts; the Oriental Hotel all potted palms and lattice work and Chinese wallpaper and grandeur contrasted with the incredibly filthy room where a girl stripper stuck two cigarettes in her vagina and puffed them. Then there was a little plump stripper with that same incredible smile. (This was the moment when the travel writer whispered to me, "How am I going to get this into my article for *House and Garden*?")

For me, Thailand was going to the floating markets down the canals and seeing everyone starting their day, brushing their teeth and their washing clothes and babies in an amazingly filthy river. Thailand was lying on the river bank in the garden of the Siam Intercontinental and seeing the ducks and geese and weeping willow trees looking like Henley on Thames. It was seeing Thais playing football with an audience of monks and waiters from the hotel. The ball fell in the river constantly and there was a boy stripped to his shorts whose job it was to retrieve it each time. Thailand was the American owner of the converted grain boat, now a beautiful restaurant, saying in wonder: "Laziness isn't considered a bad thing here, there's no translation of saving for a rainy day — a rainy day is a good day, they love the rain."

Years after this I met Mogens Bay Esbenson who cooked Thai food at Butlers Restaurant in Sydney; this is adapted from his cookery book.

Thai beef salad
(adapted from *Thai Cuisine* by Mogens Bay Esbenson [Viking O'Neil, 1986])

    1kg fillet of beef
DRESSING
    ¼ cup coriander leaves
    2 cloves garlic, crushed
    2 tbsp soy sauce
    2 tbsp lime or lemon juice

1 tbs fish sauce
1 tbs brown sugar
¼ cup chopped fresh mint
2 red onions, thinly sliced
1 punnet cherry tomatoes, halved
sweet chilli sauce to taste

Roast beef for 30 minutes or until cooked through but still rare. Slice thinly.

Mix coriander, garlic, soy sauce, juice, fish sauce and brown sugar in a food processor until well combined. Toss the sliced beef in this with chopped fresh mint, two thinly sliced red onions and a punnet of halved cherry tomatoes. Add a good slug of sweet chilli sauce.

SERVES 6

After Bangkok it was on to Melbourne but there was some problem with fuel so we had to land in Darwin. It was about 3.30am and the airport bar was in full swing. The sign over the bar read: DRESS CODE: NO STUBBIES, SINGLETS OR THONGS. I didn't have a clue what any of those things were. Lined up at the bar were several local desperadoes who Robert immediately engaged in chat. "It must be lovely living here," he said, "beautiful beaches, lovely sea to swim in." The local looked incredulous, "You can't swim here mate," he explained, as if to a particularly stupid child. "Mind you, a friend of mine took a dip, pissed he was, and when he came out of the sea he had a great dark blue shawl draped all over his head and shoulders — a Portuguese Man of War — bloody great thing, he was dead in 20 minutes."

In Melbourne we took a swish apartment in Spring Street: "A lovely air-conditioned apartment with balconies facing both ways across the city and views of the bay." Robert wrote to my mother in

February 1973: "Very smart, but so it should be at a bit more than a £100 a week. On the other hand life is expensive here and it's cheaper than the hotel. I miss the swimming pool on the roof as it's gone up to 104° and the heat knocks you down when you go out."

Robert wrote in his letters that Robin Midgeley, the director:

"...had coped very well with a fairly good cast and the play seems to go as well as ever. Business is beginning to blossom as we opened a bit quietly I think although no one bothers to send me round a return. Abbie cooked a super supper last night, kedgeree and chicken en cocotte but didn't allow quite for the enormous appetites of the 25 Aussies we had invited to say goodbye to Robin but I think everyone had enough...just. The restaurants are really very good also the food shops and supermarkets but there doesn't seem much else to buy."

In another letter he wrote:

"...the rain finally arrived and the locals are out counting the drops. Abbie gets on frightfully well with everyone and is out all the time. Did the art gallery the other afternoon, full of good French Impressionists and three Rembrandts all recently purchased. Goodness the money around. The Australian artists very fine too but Drysdale and Nolan still predominate."

On February 8: "Abbie is going to Government House for a dance tonight but Sambo (the son of old friends) is taking her and says the food will be good and they don't have to stay. Have just been to see Slaughterhouse Five *recommended by Abbie but I thought it nonsense. Also saw* The Godfather *with Abbie this time and loved it. The management have just rung up and asked if I'd do an extra matinee next week if they gave me 25% of the take but I said I didn't think so... there has been a tremendous run on tickets."*

Robin Midgeley had got the play on in Melbourne and then had to return; he ran the Leicester Playhouse. He thought he'd go home via Sydney and asked me if I'd like a weekend to see some theatre. Asking around, we were told the thing to see was David Williamson's *Don's Party*. We had a wonderful night, of course we didn't get a lot of the jokes or the local allusions but the audience found the whole thing wildly, shockingly funny and so did we. "We must go round," said Robin "and tell the actors how much we've enjoyed ourselves." I replied in a very English way that we didn't know any of them. We didn't have to wait very long for that to change because they were soon all in the tiny theatre bar with us. Robin explained who he was and who I was, and I quickly found myself saying that I would definitely bring Robert to the play when *How the Other Half Loves* got to Sydney.

The *Don's Party* cast were great fun, thoroughly enjoying being in a smash hit. Indeed, when were all in Sydney, Robert came with me to see the play and loved it. He bought the rights for London. We had a party for our cast and the *Don's Party* lot. That is how I got to meet Nick Tate, then playing Don and through him I met Charlie, the following year. So *How the Other Half Loves* and, by association *Don's Party*, changed my life.

By late February Robert and I were in Sydney with the play and staying at the Darling Point flat of an old friend.

Robert wrote home:

"It's simply lovely here but the theatre is not very comfortable with a huge orchestra pit very draughty with no air conditioning but although it's difficult to make oneself heard, we are doing about the same business as Melbourne with not quite the same enthusiasm from the locals. However social life is headlong and the girls (we had been joined by my cousin Catherine) gave a huge cocktail party last night for all the people Catherine had been instructed to look

up and some actors they'd met. Helen gave us dinner on Sunday she has a very gracious new flat in one of the old houses in Bellevue. Apparently she had had rather a time before we got there getting rid of a very drunk guest from Chicago but managed to get rid of him. She asked the local curator of museums and a rather tight lady who teaches cooking and whom I couldn't quite hear which made some of the evening a bit heavy going but the food was delicious. Two legs of lamb served simultaneously round the table. We have had two stunning days here very hot and the pool is marvellous swimming about watching the liners passing in the background. Yesterday was one of those dreadful charity luncheons, terrible pictures in the paper and all the stories wrong but rather nice women actually and quite good food. The girls managed splendidly among the hats and we got quite good champagne and chocolates to carry home."

Kedgeree

2–3 onions, finely chopped
1 tbs vegetable oil
1 tbs curry paste
1 cup rice
3–4 eggs
4 good sized salmon steaks
1 tbsp butter and enough milk to cover the fish
parsley and coriander, chopped
lemon juice
black pepper

Kedgeree is an Indian "Raj" dish so it needs a bit of spicing up. Soften onions in vegetable oil. Then add curry paste and cook, stirring, until the oil separates out and it smells fragrant. Boil rice and drain. Boil eggs until they are hardboiled, shell and chop. Purists would use smoked haddock but I prefer salmon. Either steaks or cutlets cooked in a large frying pan in milk and a little butter until the fish flakes from the bone. I buy one cutlet for every two people I'm feeding.

Put all the components parts together. Carefully heat it — don't mush it up, the oven is good for this, covered in foil. Add some butter and lots of chopped parsley and coriander, if you like it. Squeeze in lemon juice and add a lot of black pepper.

SERVES 8

Chicken en cocotte

2 tbs olive oil
20g butter
either 6–8 chicken thighs, skin on if possible or a mixture of thighs and drumsticks
12 cloves of garlic, peeled and crushed
12–15 shallots, peeled
¾ cup red wine vinegar
¾ cup tomato sauce, homemade or a good commercial brand
1½ cups chicken stock
salt and pepper
1 bay leaf
1 sprig of thyme
2 tbs flat leaf parsley, chopped

Preheat oven to 180°C.

Heat oil and butter in a casserole dish which can be used on the stove top and then go in the oven. Add the chicken in batches, cook until browned all over. Remove chicken pieces. Add garlic and shallots, cook until browned. Put chicken back, raise the heat and pour over the vinegar. It will bubble fiercely and you want to reduce it until there is hardly any left, just a coating for the chicken pieces. Add tomato sauce and stock, bay leaf, thyme and seasoning. Bring to a boil, cover and put in the oven for 30–40 minutes. Test to make sure the chicken is cooked. Stir a lump of butter in before you serve and sprinkle with the parsley.

Serve with small potatoes or crusty bread and a green salad.

SERVES 8

ROBERT AND JOAN CELEBRATING A LONG RUN

ROBERT WRITING IN THE COLT HOUSE

ABBIE (SITTING FAR LEFT) AT HURST LODGE

Chapter Ten

"WE DON'T NEED NO EDUCATION"

But of course we did. Robert's, admittedly very subjective, hatred and distrust of schools and schoolmasters coloured his whole life. It meant the three of us got very eccentric and patchy educations.

Robert, who thought life was the great educator, had finished his schooling at 16. This was when my grandfather's finances suffered yet another downturn and Robert was summoned to the headmaster's study at Wellington and given a one-way ticket to London. He stood on the railway station platform, pinching himself to persuade himself this wasn't a dream. Years later, when he was famous and successful, Wellington asked Robert to return and present the prizes at speech day; Robert agreed to come back on the condition that he could burn the place down. At Wellington he was beaten and bullied and made miserable by the cold, the dreadful food, the pointlessness of lessons. He said of himself:

"I was an unattractive child, made to feel even more so; a stupid child

never allowed to forget it; an idle child, to be whipped; a greedy child, to be starved; a friendless child, to be shunned; an eager-to-please child, to be snubbed."

From *Robert Morley: Responsible Gentleman* by Robert Morley and Sewell Stokes (Heinemann, 1966) p. 28.

The only thing which got him through the years at Wellington was his conviction that he would be an actor. On a half day holiday from his prep school he had wandered into a matinee performance of Shaw's play *The Doctor's Dilemma*. Shaw's anti hero, Dudedat, an artist, has a great speech in which he justifies his life (as he is dying):

"... I haven't always been able to live up to my ideal. But in my own real world I have never done anything wrong, never denied my faith, never been untrue to myself. I've been threatened and blackmailed and insulted and starved... And now's it's all over there's an indescribable peace. I believe in Michael Angelo, Velasquez, and Rembrandt; in the might of design, the mystery of colour, the redemption of all things by Beauty everlasting, and the message of Art that has made these hands blessed."

Robert's world turned upside down that afternoon, as *"the magic of Shaw turned me from a fat, unlikable, bewildered teenager into a potential leading man who wanted to walk the road that Shaw indicated. I never wavered after that in my intention to go on the stage."*

From *Robert Morley: Responsible Gentleman* by Robert Morley and Sewell Stokes (Heinemann, 1966) p. 26.

All his contemporaries at Wellington were destined for the army and when Robert told the masters he was going on the stage, they were furious. He never spoke of his school days unless it was to stress how unhappy he had been. We were also never allowed to watch *Tom Brown's Schooldays* if he was in the room.

Rupert House

The first school for all of us was Rupert House in Henley. It was run almost on the lines of a dame school. The eccentric headmistress, Janet Densham, was a chain smoker who would absentmindedly tap her cigarette ash onto our heads as she spoke to us. My mother always knew if I had had a session with Miss Densham as she could smell my smoky hair. We were asked every day at morning assembly if we were staying for lunch because children who lived near enough the school would walk home for lunch.

One particular day I found myself answering "No", when asked whether I would be there for lunch. About a mile from Henley was an excellent restaurant called Chez Peter, where Robert would take us all for Sunday lunch sometimes. I decided that day I would walk up the hill to this restaurant and have my lunch there.

At Chez Peter the waiters would flambé anything they could. The food always slightly tasted of the paraffin used to fuel the burner under the chafing dish but that seemed to add to its flavour. Robert often had steak Diane which was cooked alongside the table, on a trolley, with much flourishing of bottles of brandy and swirling of frying pans. Crepes suzettes were often the pudding of choice and although I really preferred pancakes sans alcohol, the spectacular flames made the whole thing into a wonderful performance.

On this particular day at school, when 12.30 came I was somehow allowed out into the Henley streets on my own and tagged along with a little boy in my class called George Wynne Wilson. He lived near the river and when he heard I was intending to walk all the way up the hill to Chez Peter he chivalrously suggested I come home with him. His mother must have been a bit surprised but she didn't say anything. Frankly lunch was a bit of a disappointment and after it, Mrs Wynne Wilson took us back for afternoon classes. She must have had a word to someone at school.

I was picked up by our nanny, Nancy Stubbs, because my mother was in London for the day. However, I remember Joan sitting on my bed that evening, dressed in her London clothes and gently enquiring what earth I had been thinking of to say I wasn't staying at school for lunch. I told her about the plan to walk to Chez Peter and I remember her turning away to hide her amusement and then giving me a serious talk about the dangers of little girls of six roaming the streets by themselves. I could actually have walked all the way. After all I only had to cross one small road and the world was a much safer one in the early 1950s. Whether or not the restaurant would have given me lunch or not is a moot point but I suppose my mother saw some sort of adventurous spirit in this scheme, as well as an inherited love of restaurants or at least delicious food.

At Rupert House a rather severe woman called Mrs Hart Davis (Comfort was her not too appropriate first name) taught English, geography, French and art. At ten and a half my report from her was that in reading, comprehension and language:

"... she excels as her vocabulary is very good for her age and she shows a natural interest in words and great enjoyment of poetry and stories. On paper she can express herself readily and when she takes the trouble to reflect, she writes good compositions but sometimes she is too easily satisfied and produces baby-ish work not worthy of her ability."

In my report on art she wrote, no doubt accurately:

"Annabel has no great manual dexterity but by using her intelligence

and observation she has improved her drawing considerably. In her case teaching is rewarding and she gets much enjoyment out of painting as she has good taste and feeling for colour."

I didn't shine at needlework and although I tried very hard to sing in tune "it didn't come easily". Not much changes, 50-something years on I love needlework, but I'm still trying unsuccessfully to sing in tune. For the spring term in 1957, when I had been absent for 30 days out of 52, Mrs Hart Davis wrote sharply that "of the little work Annabel has accomplished this term, some has been good and some astonishingly incompetent. I can only conclude that she has too many distractions and that at times her work takes last place in a heavy schedule." The headmistress (Miss Densham having retired, it was now a Miss Sylvia Fawcett) wrote: "Whilst sympathetic to the claims of family events, I must emphasise that too frequent interruptions to school routines are distracting for the pupil and difficult for the teacher." I find it fascinating, in view of the inordinate amount of praise that is bestowed on modern children, that our school reports were quite brutally honest. I can't think that today many ten year olds' work would be described as "astonishingly incompetent" without complaints from their indulgent parents.

By the time I was about to leave Rupert House, Mrs Hart Davis had been replaced by a Mrs Barnicot who I obviously irritated enormously. She wrote that in history I did well "… when her rather fitful attention is caught, at other times she amuses herself, usually by distracting her neighbour." On my geography report she wrote a trifle gnomically "she needs to learn that an interest can be acquired even in that which is not obviously interesting."

One of my classmates was Susannah Piper, the daughter of the artist John Piper and his librettist wife Myfanwy. Theirs was a bohemian household and when Susannah came for a sleep over, my mother spent hours brushing and combing and untangling the knots in her hair. My best friends were Corinne Stokes and Fanny Van Namen, whose mother was American and reed thin and elegant. Fanny's father was very high up in the biscuit firm Huntley and Palmers and he organised a school outing around the biscuit-making factory in Reading. The smell of the warm biscuit dough infused the air and we were given huge paper bags full of broken biscuits to munch. Beautiful tins full of beautiful biscuits were Christmas presents from the Van Namens. When I later went to Reading Technical College, a hop, skip and jump from H and P's, that glorious smell of baking dough would tantalise us as we sat in economic history lectures.

Fast forward to 2005, Bikaner, Rajasthan where in an Aladdin's cave of a shop the owner proudly showed us a Huntley and Palmer's biscuit tin label with a naïve drawing of the factory circa 1890.

Corinne and her two older sisters lived in Wargrave village, in Ferry Lane, practically in the River Thames. Her gentle mother Kay was bringing the girls up alone as Michael North, a composer and musician had died young; he was physically very like my father, large and expansive and his shocking sudden death brought me to the realisation that it wasn't only the old who died.

But of course we couldn't stay at Rupert House forever. Searching for a school for Sherry, Robert put an advertisement in the personal column of *The Times*. He was a father with gruesome memories of his own school days looking for somewhere to send his son where the standards of comfort and food were that of a good three star hotel.

Sizewell Hall

Robert visited many schools and finally settled on one in Suffolk, Sizewell Hall. This is Robert's first favourable impression of Sizewell, in a letter to Granny Morley:

> *"The house has its own private beach of a mile and really wonderful grounds and there are only 37 children, boys and girls and a very young staff headed by a Dutchman who I liked on sight and who, like me, doesn't think much of cricket and endless hours spent in organised games. He does keep the children well fed and it's the only school I struck where they can have second helpings of everything at all meals and where they produce their own magazine without a mention of second elevens and seem to preserve their individuality and sense of humour and to be really friendly with the staff. There seems an atmosphere of tolerance about the whole place...they have films every Sunday and no church unless they want to go. I have seen a dozen schools in all and am more convinced than ever that most children never recover their sense of humour and individuality after an English boarding school. I do hope he will not be miserable, I don't think he will."*

When Sherry was about 14 or 15 Harry Tuyn got bored of running a boys' prep school and decided the money would be better running a girls' finishing school in Switzerland. He took Sherry and the local doctor's son with him and coached them for Oxbridge. Successfully.

Hurst Lodge

When I turned 11 the search was on for a school for me. I only remember Joan and I looking at two: Elmhurst and Hurst Lodge. Elmhurst, which was a ballet/theatre school where the Mills girls, Juliet and Hayley, were pupils, was the first one. Hayley, who was by then a child star after her performance in *Tiger Bay* and who was sporty and slightly hearty in aertex shirt and shorts, showed me around. My mother was (rightly as it turned out) suspicious of the

Principal's middle aged son, who wore a cassock and sat in on the interview.

Hurst Lodge was therefore the school we settled on. It was founded, owned and run by Doris Stainer who was the sister of Leslie Howard, the casting agent Irene Howard and the actor Arthur Howard. Doris seemed much tougher and more forceful than the rather weedy Leslie, or rather than Leslie's screen persona, Ashley Wilkes in *Gone With The Wind*, who seemed ready to be dominated, not only by Scarlett but even by the sweet Melanie. Arthur was a side-kick to a rather horrible man called Jimmy Edwards, who played a cane-wielding schoolmaster in a TV series called *Wacko*. Doris was a little plump pouter pigeon of a woman with red hair, always very smartly dressed in tweed and cashmere in winter and silk dresses in the summer. She had hankered after a career in the ballet, which she was mad about. (I have never quite been able to see the point of ballet; I see it as the opposite of opera, in which, if someone wants to say something they do so very slowly and at least three times. In ballet I just long for them to speak. Tell him you've been turned into a swan, for God's sake, I want to scream. The whole thing seems a bit perverse.)

At Hurst Lodge we all had to learn ballet with its arcane positions and dress code, we wore something called a "cross-over", a knitted bolero, over our sickly turquoise coloured ballet tunics. Hard to believe it now but I could actually go "en pointe" up on my salmon pink satin encased toes, thanks to having a second toe as long as my big toe. We also learnt tap and something called "Stage" which was modern ballet. I was hopeless at all of these. On the academic side, as much as there was one, there was the headmistress, Agnes Russell. She was deaf and sported two large hearing aids covered up by a pink or blue scarf which she wore as a bandeau round her head. There was a French Mam'zelle who taught us French, wore sandals and had bare, brown rather hairy legs on show in summer. And then there was the English teacher, Miss Noreen Milne.

Miss Milne was an inspirational teacher; she commented that my approach to literature "reveals imagination and perception but she must make more effort with her written work." By the time I was 13 she thought I had "combated a tendency to let things slide." At 15 she thought that if I exerted myself more I would do better.

When she announced that she was leaving to get married we were not surprised. At the previous sports day she had made herself a white, raw silk "sack dress" and pinned a bunch of lilies of the valley to the shoulder. The fathers buzzed around her like wasps round a pot of jam.

I especially hated games. Netball in winter was presided over by a dragon of a games mistress, Mrs Higgins, and was a kind of torture. Just as I don't understand ballet, I don't understand ball games. I'm sure they equate to some sort of tribal necessity for a blood sport, a gladiatorial contest but I find them baffling and the people who don't play them but only watch them, incomprehensible. I'll grant you tennis obviously requires skill, strength and extremely good hand to eye coordination; all qualities my fairy godmother at birth seems to have decided I shouldn't possess.

The only way to get out of games was to have a note signed by one's mother to say you had your period. I got my mother to sign a pile of notes which I dated as appropriate. If Mrs Higgins thought I was a biological anomaly who menstruated three weeks out of four, she never challenged me, only writing on my report: "Must definitely make an effort to attend more often." Some chance. If you were "off games" it was as well to lie low, otherwise some bossy prefect would find you something to do. Those of us who had managed to get out of games gathered in one of the bathrooms, sitting in a row on the edge of the bath and gossiping.

Ever the indulgent parent, Robert, encouraged by me, who said how much nicer school would be if we had a pool to swim in, was the first subscriber to a parent-funded swimming pool at Hurst Lodge. It was built for £2500 and opened by him and John Neville — described as a 35-year-old Shakespearian actor — on a rainy day in the summer of 1960. Robert was making a film of Oscar Wilde and John Neville was playing Bosie to his Oscar. One notice unkindly described John Neville as the oldest undergraduate Oxford had ever had and of course he was at least 15 years too old to play Alfred Douglas, and Robert was a bit too old to play Wilde.

Another film was being made at the same time, starring Peter Finch. This was made in Technicolour, whereas Robert's version was black and white. Finch's is the version that pops up most on TV as *The Trials of Oscar Wilde*. Robert's version had Ralph Richardson playing Carson, the prosecuting counsel and my brother Wilton in one scene playing Wilde's son, Cyril. For us, his children, it was a chance to see Robert in one of the great roles of his career. By the end of shooting the money had run out and the film was in danger of never being completed. Robert's final scene as Wilde features him sitting at a café table in France, at the end of his life. It was shot in close up — cheap and, I imagine, quick to film. Robert's final speech is imbued with the wit and the humanity of Wilde and the pathos of shame and exile that Sewell Stokes captured in the original play.

There are photographs from various newspapers of the three of us, Robert, John Neville and me at the official opening of the pool. Robert and John Neville are sitting on the diving board and I am standing beside them. I look positively middle-aged for almost 15, huge in my shirt-waister dress, cardigan and court shoes, with an unbecoming hair style and a glum expression.

One thing I did like at school was something called "Extra Drama" which was taught by two visiting teachers Miss Jones and Miss Hudson. I realise now they were a couple; Miss Elaine Hudson, older, gentler and calmer and Miss Bess Jones, who was a feisty red head. They prepared us for the Guildhall School Exams.

I seem to have got to Grade Three. In the Poetry Society exams, at 15, I did the speech of Juliet's nurse from Romeo and Juliet as well as one of Ismene's speeches from Anouilh's *Antigone*. The examiner's comment was "intelligent careful work with talented and inspired interpretation."

When I started at Hurst Lodge, I was intensely home-sick, crying all the way home from school on Friday afternoons and all the way back to school on Monday mornings. Robert said I used to say goodbye to them on Monday mornings as if I was never going to see them again. My diary entries for Monday mornings usually start "back to the dump" or "back to prison". Decades later, driving down the road that we used to take I was overcome with a feeling of intense dread; there was a point, a sharpish left hand turn when I would contemplate opening the car door and letting myself fall out. I never quite dared to do it although I did once chain myself to the front door handle of the house with my bicycle chain and a padlock.

Sometimes I managed not to go back to school but to stay at home with some vague ailment. Once I almost too successfully faked appendicitis; Joan came to school and collected me. She got a second opinion from our family doctor, Dr Black, who thought it was more likely to be indigestion — probably from the food which was spectacularly awful. We had puddings called Angel Delight, butterscotch flavour or a pink one known as Elizabeth Arden's Face Cream. There was also a version of bread and butter pudding which was truly nasty and a "curry" which was a bright yellow mush of chewy lumps of meat in a sauce made with curry powder. The school cook must have just stirred in tablespoonfuls of neat curry powder — no frying of the spices first. The "curry" was served with sliced bananas and raisins. Toad in the Hole was gristly sausages and flabby batter; a world away from my mother's ambrosial Yorkshire pudding.

From hate to love

As everything else about us changes as we age, so does our taste in food. Things that revolted me as a child I now enjoy. Nobody in the family liked beetroot and though I think I sometimes came across it in a jar of vinegar, I never ate beetroot until I came to Australia. There it was always in a "real" hamburger, bleeding all over the lettuce and into the bun. But the wonderful complex and sweet taste of baked beetroot makes it one of the best vegetables to eat.

Roast beetroot

> beetroot
> olive oil
> salt and pepper

Pre-heat oven to 200°C.

Smear scrubbed and dried beets with olive oil, season with salt and pepper and wrap in foil. Bake as you would a jacket potato, a medium-sized beetroot can take an hour in a hot oven. When cool enough to handle, peel.

Allow one beetroot per person or less if the beetroot are very large.

I like mine smeared with Dijonnaise (half mayonnaise, half Dijon mustard.)

Although I love beetroot hot, it is wonderful in a salad. It seems to have an affinity with smoked or pickled fish, with eggs, apples and potatoes.

Herring, apple and beetroot salad

> 2–3 Matjes herrings (the ones in the refrigerated section of the supermarket are the best)
> 2 crisp apples
> 3–4 small boiled potatoes
> 2–3 beetroot
> 2 hard boiled eggs
>
> DRESSING
> 2 tbsp of vinaigrette*
> 1 tbsp mayonnaise
> 1 tbsp sour cream or yoghurt
> 2 tbsp dill and or parsley or chives, chopped

I always make a vinaigrette as G did, equal quantities of olive oil and wine vinegar, either red or white, salt and pepper, a crushed clove of garlic, a pinch of sugar and a teaspoon of grainy mustard. Make in a screw top jar and store in the fridge.

Snip two or three herring fillets into pieces. Chop and core the apple. Slice the potatoes and stir these into the dressing. Peel and dice the beetroot and dress in a little vinaigrette. Chop the eggs. Put the herring mixture in the middle of a shallow bowl, arrange the beetroot around the edge and put the eggs on top and then the herbs.

As you serve it or your guests serve themselves, the whole thing will become a pink melange but at least, as my nanny would have said, "You've started out tidy."

SERVES 4

I hated all milk puddings, but tapioca was the worst: "frog's spawn". Semolina was also pretty horrible — at school a smear of ersatz jam was added. Rice pudding revolted me. However, semolina-based pasta is something I am happy to experience.

For ages I have been attempting to make gnocchi, unsuccessfully. I bought a potato ricer while in New Zealand, used it once and found the effort involved in making potato gnocchi from scratch simply not worth it BUT then I found a recipe for three cheese semolina gnocchi, which was quick and easy. Fried sage leaves and melted butter are a good addition, when you serve it.

Semolina gnocchi

750ml milk
1 cup semolina
3 egg yolks
150g taleggio cheese, rind removed and chopped
salt and pepper
1 tbsp chopped marjoram or thyme
½ cup grated mozzarella
½ cup grated parmesan

Put the milk in a large saucepan and bring to the boil. Whisk in the semolina and stir it with a wooden spoon for 2–3 minutes (it will become very thick). Remove from heat and add egg yolks and taleggio, salt and pepper. Combine well and spread into a lightly greased shallow tin. Chill in the fridge for an hour or two then cut into small rectangles (4cm x 10cm) and place on a lightly greased oven tray. Sprinkle with the herbs and mozzarella and parmesan. Grill until the cheese is melted, it will sit in a warm oven quite happily until you are ready to serve.

SERVES 4–5

Semifreddo and panna cotta

I suppose what Lizzie Arden's face cream was aiming at was some delicious little sweet, creamy, light end to a meal. These panna cottas can be made in individual cups or glasses, easy to serve and pretty; the semifreddos work best made in loaf tins but can be made in advance and frozen.

In Sicily a few years ago, our friend Tony was always on the lookout for a semifreddo; his enquiry was inevitably met with a shrug and a "Scusi" — no semifreddi, not even for ready money. Heavenly things, half way between an ice cream and a mousse, they are as easy as pie to make.

Semifreddo al torrone (Nougat semifreddo)
(adapted from *Delicious*, March 2013)

> ¼ cup marsala
> ⅔ cup castor sugar
> 2 eggs, separated plus 1 yolk
> 200g torrone (hard almond nougat) chilled then finely chopped
> 300ml thickened cream, whipped

Whisk marsala, sugar and three egg yolks in a heatproof bowl over simmering water until thick. Set aside to cool. Whisk the two eggwhites until soft peaks form. Add the nougat to the marsala mixture and stir through gently. Fold in whipped cream and lastly egg whites. Divide mixture among six 200ml glasses or put the lot into a loaf tin. Freeze 4–6 hours.

This is very good served with poached cherries or figs.

SERVES 6

Crunchy lime semifreddo
(adapted from *Delicious*, Dec 2010/Jan 2011)

395g can sweetened condensed milk
finely grated zest and juice of 6 limes (you need ¾ cup or 185ml lime juice)
300ml pure (thin) cream
150g ginger thin biscuits finely crushed
sliced mango and mint leaves to garnish

Lightly oil and line a 1.6-litre loaf tin with plastic wrap, leaving plenty overhanging. Pour condensed milk into a bowl and stir in lime juice and zest, the mixture will start to thicken. Set aside. In another bowl whisk cream to soft peaks and then fold into condensed milk mixture. Spoon a quarter of mixture into the prepared tin, level the surface and then sprinkle over one quarter of the biscuit crumbs, gently shaking the pan until evenly spread. Place pan in freezer ten minutes until set. Repeat process three more times, ending with layer of biscuit crumbs. Cover tin with plastic wrap. Refrigerate in freezer 6–8 hours or overnight.

To serve, unwrap, invert over a serving dish and remove tin, then unwrap and slice. Serve with slices of mango and mint leaves.

SERVES 8

Panna cotta is literally "cooked cream" or cream with the addition of flavouring and gelatine to make it set. Delicate, rich and with a wonderful texture, the trick is not too much gelatine, these little delights are a perfect end to a meal. There is much written now about gelatine leaves and how superior they are to the powdered stuff, I'd say don't bother with them, powdered is fine in my book — and this *is* my book, after all.

Panna cotta

300ml thickened (double) cream
600ml thin (single) cream
180g castor sugar
A vanilla bean, split (you can always substitute a teaspoon of vanilla)
3 tsp or 1 sachet gelatine

Place the creams in a saucepan with the sugar and the vanilla bean, split and with the seeds scaped into the cream. Cook over low heat stirring to dissolve the sugar, bring to a gentle simmer and remove from the heat. Dissolve the gelatine in 2 tablespoons of water in a small pan over low heat and stir into the cream. Pour the mixture into 6 small (150ml) moulds and refrigerate at least 4 hours.

Run the blade of a knife round the edge of the mould to facilitate turning out and serve with roasted plums.

SERVES 6

Roasted plums

500g dark plums, halved and stones removed
80g castor sugar
1 vanilla bean
1 cinnamon stick
juice of 1 lemon

Place plums in a single layer in a shallow baking dish and pour over sugar. Put in vanilla bean and cinnamon stick. Add the juice of a lemon and a little water. Bake at 180°C for about 20–25 minutes or until cooked. Cover and refrigerate.

Honey and raspberry panna cotta

(The raspberry component of this is a puree that sits on the top of the panna cotta, if you are going to turn the panna cottas out, remember not to put the raspberry layer on until you serve them.)

> 2 cups (500ml) thickened cream
> ⅔ cup (240g) honey
> 1 rounded tsp powdered gelatine
> 250g raspberries
> juice of 1 lemon
> 1–2 tbsp icing sugar

Place cream and honey in a saucepan and warm over low heat, stirring to combine. Dissolve gelatine in hot water in a small saucepan and stir in cream mixture. Divide among six 200ml glasses or ramekins and refrigerate until set. Place the raspberries and the lemon juice in a blender and whizz into a smooth puree. Sieve and discard the seeds. Stir the icing sugar through. Spoon the sauce over the top of each panna cotta either in the glasses or, if you turn out the panna cottas, over the top, once on the plate.

SERVES 6

Finishing school

It was traditional at girls' boarding schools to have crushes on the older girls: Margaret Don, Anne Evans and a girl called Anne Shelmedine were my favourite seniors.

In 1960 a director called Peter Dews made all Shakespeare's histories into a television series: *An Age of Kings*. Tim (Robert) Hardy had fallen in love with my aunt, Sally. He played Prince Hal who becomes Henry V. He cut his hair in the pudding basin shape, shown in all representations of the young Henry V. Because it was educational, the seniors were allowed to stay up and watch it on television. I claimed kinship with Tim and was allowed to stay up and watch too.

The previous summer Tim had been at Stratford in the great season that included Paul Robeson playing Othello. Tim played Oberon in a production of *A Midsummer Night's Dream* that is imprinted on my mind's eye. Designed by Lila di Nobili and directed by Peter Hall, it starred Charles Laughton as Bottom and Judi Dench as Titania with the young and suitably tall Vanessa Redgrave as Helena. Robert and Joan took me to Stratford to see both *Othello* and *A Midsummer Night's Dream* and we went to visit Tim and Sally in their Stratford cottage.

I had a huge crush on Tim and his presence at weekend teas at "Barn Elms" was always a bonus. From initially not really approving of him as a partner for Sally — he was married with a small son — G had come to accept him and love him, as she did Robert. She spoke to both of them, though, rather as she does to Rex Harrison in *My Fair Lady*. There was always that note of slight exasperation. Having lived independently of a man for the years in the war when my grandfather was away fighting and then when they divorced, she was used to taking care, not only of herself, but of her dependents, her sister Gracie and her son Johnny in particular. Running a house, earning money and providing a home to the extended family, all this fell to her and she rose to the challenge. Throughout her life she was an energised force; my father said it was unwise to sit, let alone, settle onto a sofa when she was around. If you did, she would almost certainly want to move it to another position. In the last days of her life when my friend Christopher Matthew phoned her and commented that she sounded a little breathless (she was dying of lung cancer), she said it was probably because she'd just been moving the piano.

Back at Hurst Lodge, life had improved by the time I was a senior, I had good friends and was "popular", particularly when I took a group of class mates to see Robert in *Majority of One*.

Majority of One was a really strange choice for Robert; he played a Japanese businessman who falls in love with a Jewish widow. The widow was played by an American actress, Molly Picon. Robert wore a kimono and made some attempt to make his eyes look vaguely Asian. However, as when he played the Emperor of China in the film of *Genghis Khan*, credulity had to be suspended by the onlookers. Alan Tagg designed the set, all sliding paper panels and Tatami matting. Alan Tagg was a wonderful designer who could equally handle designing for the Royal Court, as his obituary said "in mould, rubble and drab shades", as he could designing for stars like Ingrid Bergman, Deborah Kerr and Maggie Smith in West End and Chichester productions. He was Robert's first choice of designer whether Robert was producing or acting in plays and he became a friend, coming to dinner with Charlie and me in London in the late seventies and early eighties, with his partner, Charles. The gentlest and most softy spoken of men, Robert called him "whispering Alan Tagg", he loved spending time in his house in rural France near Uzes, which he once leant to Ros Chatto and me.

I took my group of friends back stage after the matinee where we had a meal (spaghetti and white wine) with the cast and crew. Robert had instigated a tradition that everyone would eat together between the two shows on a Saturday — not only the cast but also the stage hands, stage manager and assistant stage manager, the wardrobe mistress and the dressers. Ros Chatto cooked these backstage meals, lugging vast amounts of food in a taxi from her house in Chelsea across London to the West End.

I couldn't wait to leave Hurst Lodge and did so smartly after my sixteenth birthday. I had a few GCE "O" Levels and one "A" in

THE ICING ON THE CAKE

English; I was the first person to take an "A" level exam at the school which gives you an idea of the academic standards. Miss Milne having left, her replacement was a large sad lady who was obviously having a nervous breakdown. I was told that if I wanted to take the "A" level in English, I would have to do it on my own. I scraped through and then went to Reading Technical College to take some more "O" levels and the English "A" level again (see chapter 11). Another GCE that I passed, much to everyone's surprise, was Art. I put it down to the wonderful way I painted empty milk bottles in my still life composition.

I never felt that I had had a "proper" education and spent years feeling that my life would have been quite different if I had been to university. However, when I finally went to Sydney University in the 1990s I was staggered that there were people embarking on an English degree who had never even heard of Ovid.

UNCLE TIM HARDY AS PRINCE HAL/HENRY V IN
AN AGE OF KINGS (1960)

ME LOOKING SOULFUL — ABOUT TO EMBARK ON AN ACTING CAREER

ROS CHATTO, A GREAT COOK AND A GREAT FRIEND FOR OVER 60 YEARS

Chapter Eleven

ECCENTRIC EMPLOYMENT

Further education and the discovery of boys

At Reading Tech we were treated as adults and tried to act like it. There were boys in duffle coats and scarves and my friend Gussie and I would leave Tech, go into the ladies loo in Heelas, the local department store, hoick up our skirts and pull down our (black) jumpers, backcomb our hair into beehives and put on pale lipstick. Then we were ready for the local coffee bars and the pubs. I remember Ray Charles singing "But you don't know me" and Elvis singing how maybe he didn't love me as he should have, on the juke box. Gussie found a lover and ran away with him, but I was more nervous. At my seventeenth birthday party some of the guests threw bread into the pool, to my father's disgust, and a certain amount of sexual activity took place in the woods and the more secluded bits of the garden.

On a cold clear Christmas Eve, a whole group of us walked the mile from the village to "Fairmans", arm in arm and singing carols, while shooting stars streaked above us. We sat around the sitting room fireplace, on the floor, and toasted bread on toasting forks. I wasn't sure who I loved most: John who had a motorbike, Terry who was funny or David who was bearded and going to be a painter. One night, for reasons I have now forgotten, David and I set out for a party and ended up stranded at a country railway station. The station master unlocked the waiting room for us and then went home. We sat all through the freezing night, talking and occasionally kissing, waiting for the "milk" train which came through about 5.30 in the morning. When David went to study art in Newcastle he wrote me letters in his beautiful handwriting with descriptions of places he had been and paintings he was doing.

The most exotic men around Reading were two Australians: Dave and Eric who periodically went off to do Voluntary Service Overseas. Eric was the archetypical Australian, blond and with blue eyes that seemed used to gazing into the far distance. Dave was dark and bearded. I really fancied Eric more than Dave but they shared everything including their girlfriends so I went out with them both. Eric went to Algeria to put in a water supply for a village and wrote me a love letter. Dave and I went to Paris, because he was going off via France to do some more VSO work and Robert was making a film there. We had a meal with some friends of Dave's and Eric's in Fulham, travelled overnight to France on the ferry from Dover and then took the train to Gare du Nord, where I got a taxi to the Hotel Brighton, Robert's suite and luxury.

London and feeding a crowd

After Tech I had to find some sort of a job so I went to live in London, in the house of my friends the Chattos.

I met Ros Chatto when she carried me screaming and kicking out of a café called the SF Café, aged four. She took me back to

Robert's dressing room and told me to behave myself. We had come to join him for a meal between shows during the run of *The Little Hut* when Ros was the Assistant Stage Manager. Ros and Tom, her husband and Gran, her mother, and a bit later on, her two sons, James and Daniel became my second family. By the time I went to live in their house in Chelsea, when I first left home at 17, Ros had become a successful theatrical agent; her clients were, among others: Sarah Miles, Felicity Kendal, Susan Hampshire and Angharad Rees. Later on, she was Paul Schofield's agent as well as Alan Bennett's and, of course, Robert's. The sitting room in the little house in Christchurch Street was always full of people, both clients and friends. Ros was always totally protective and endlessly encouraging to her clients. She was a great provider: advice, comfort and sustenance. She was also an inspired and inspirational cook.

Ros would come in from the office with carrier bags bulging with food she had bought at lunch time or on the way home and immediately start cooking. Her mother, known to everyone of Ros's generation as "Mummy" and to my generation as "Gran", would be in the kitchen, washing up or pottering about. She had ulcers so she lived on a very restricted diet: endless cups of tea and something called Bengers, often with a rich tea biscuit (a misnomer if ever there was one). Gran made the most exquisitely thin slices of white bread and butter, which were always on offer. Ros would come in like a whirlwind and, if I was there and the boys home from school, we would somehow all pack into the kitchen to pitch in and help. There was always a choice of things to eat. She would put a bowl of fruit on the table, in the sitting room, which was where we ate. Ros's fruit bowls were like "still lives" — cornucopias. This was so unlike "Fairmans" where my mother meticulously divided the fruit up into different bowls and we never had bread on the table; Ros always put out a loaf and a slab of butter.

Ros could cook anything; the only thing Gran was better at

cooking was pastry, so *she* made the pastry for any pie or a tart. Tom had an Anglo-Indian background so curries were a feature. Because Ros was usually cooking for a crowd things were made in large quantities in a huge orangey-red Le Creuset casserole dish.

It was here that I learnt that there are some things which can't be made in small quantities, one of which is bollito misto. A true bollito misto has ingredients like a calf's head and a pickled ox tongue in it — you won't get far asking for those in your local supermarket. So the recipe below is an adaptation. It is, of course, worth hunting down the Cotechino sausage.

Bollito misto

1 piece of gravy beef (about 1.3kg)
a whole chicken or two breast fillets and two thigh fillets
4 coarse Italian pork sausages
2 bunches Dutch carrots
15 small onions
15–20 small potatoes
1 Cotechino sausage (pre-cooked)

BROTH
2 large carrots
2 stalks celery
some parsley, thyme and bay leaves
3 cloves
black peppercorns
pinch of salt

Put the broth vegetables, herbs, cloves and peppercorns in a large stockpot with plenty of cold water and bring to the boil. Put in the beef and simmer for an hour and a half and then add the chicken and sausages.

Cook for a further hour if using a whole chicken. Remove the broth vegetables and add trimmed Dutch carrots, onions and potatoes. Simmer until tender.

Heat the Cotechino in water in a separate pan. When ready to serve, carve the chicken and the beef, slice the sausages and serve on the largest platter you have, with the vegetables. Soup plates are good, so everyone has the broth as well.

SERVES 12

A traditional accompaniment to bollito misto is salsa verde. Below is my favourite version.

Salsa verde

> 40g flat parsley leaves
> 20g fresh basil
> 20g rocket
> 2 cloves crushed garlic
> 1 tbsp capers, drained
> 1 tbsp cornichons or gherkins
> 4 anchovy fillets
> 1 tbsp Dijon mustard
> 1 tbsp red wine vinegar
> 100ml olive oil
> ground black pepper

Pulse or chop all ingredients to make a glossy bright green sauce. Keep covered and serve with the bollito misto.

Risotto is a very versatile dish, you can add chicken or prawns to the one below or perhaps some mixed mushrooms. Portobello, brown and Chanterelle mushrooms fried in butter make a good addition just prior to serving. Oven risotto is so easy, none of that boring stirring — I never cook it any other way these days.

Oven risotto

2 tbsp olive oil
1 onion, finely chopped
150g streaky bacon, finely chopped (leave this out for a vegetarian option)
2 cloves crushed garlic
2 leeks, trimmed and sliced
2 carrots, diced or thinly sliced
large handful of chopped parsley
340g risotto (Arborio) rice
175ml white wine
2L hot vegetable or chicken stock
OPTIONAL: 400g tin small brown or green lentils, rinsed and drained
100g grated Parmesan, plus more to serve

Heat oven to 170°C. Heat olive oil in a large heavy-based flame-proof casserole dish with a lid. Add onion and bacon and fry a few minutes. Reduce heat and stir in garlic, leeks, carrots and half the parsley. Add the rice and stir to coat for 2–3 minutes before adding the wine. Let it bubble and then add the stock and season with salt and pepper, bring to a simmer and stir well. Then put the lid on and put it in the oven for 20 minutes.

Add lentils if you wish and cook another 10 minutes. Stir in parmesan and season well.

SERVES 4 GENEROUSLY

Elizabeth David describes cassoulet as "...a genuine, abundant, earthy richly flavoured and patiently simmered dish of the ideal farmhouse kitchen."

From *A Book of Mediterranean Food* by Elizabeth David (Penguin, 1950).

Traditionally this Toulousain dish would have preserved goose, pig's feet and perhaps a piece of mutton as some of its ingredients. It's probably better to cook the haricot beans from scratch, I have used tinned ones in the past but it really needs the long cooking time and tinned beans will turn to mush. It's a lunch rather than a supper dish and needs to be served with a green salad and bread to mop up the juices.

Cassoulet

750g haricot beans, soaked overnight
1 clove garlic
thyme
1 onion
bay leaf
quantity of fresh breadcrumbs
1 duck, roasted
500g coarse pork sausages
250g streaky bacon, chopped

Cook the beans in plenty of water with the onion, garlic, bacon and herbs. When the beans are tender, drain them but keep the cooking liquid. Meanwhile roast the duck in a hot oven for an hour and grill or fry the sausages and bacon. Layer the beans and the meats in a deep pot. An earthenware 'cassoulet' is traditional but any oven proof dish will do. Add enough liquid to come about half way up the pot and cover with a layer of breadcrumbs. Cook in a slow oven, a crust will form on top as it cooks. Stir this into the dish and sprinkle on more breadcrumbs, repeating the process over a couple of hours.

SERVES 6–8

The other area of my life where Ros was a great influence was that she, unlike my mother Joan, was a great reader. I loved being read to as a child and made my mother read *The Secret Garden* to me before I learnt to read. But nothing was as exciting as when I was suddenly able to read for myself. Then there was Beatrix Potter, terrifying Mr Tod and poor Tom Kitten being made into a suet pudding by those awful rats and the gentler Alison Uttley. My mother's childhood books, which I inherited, included George MacDonald's *At the Back of The North Wind* and a set of the wonderful illustrated books by Arthur Rackham. There was a *Cinderella*, which was illustrated entirely in silhouettes, except for the front plate which showed the motherless Ella under a tree in a garden, about to meet her Fairy Godmother for the first time. Anyone who has seen Rackham's illustrations thinks of his extraordinary trees, twisted into tortured shapes. Having looked at his illustrations you hurried home just a bit faster on a walk through the woods as dusk fell on a winter afternoon, thinking all the time of those Rackham-esque branches ready to encircle a passing traveller.

Much less dark than Rackham was Milly Molly Mandy who lived in a village very like Wargrave, in a house that was very like the ones in Crazies Hill, a thatched cottage. Her mother and aunt wore the same clothes that our cooks and "dailies" wore and the old ladies in the stories looked like my paternal grandmother, Daisy Fass in her shapeless dark, ankle-length clothes. Milly Molly Mandy herself wore smocked dresses and short white socks and cardigans, like I and my friends did, went blackberrying and to parties and played with her little friend Susan. Billy Brown was like the boy who lived opposite us at the farm, Dennis Loder.

Ros and Tom's house was crammed with books; Ros leant me the wonderful picaresque *Anthony Adverse* by Herbert Allen and a book called *The Heart of Jade* which was about the Aztecs or just possibly the Incas. Somehow Ros's copy got lost and I was delighted when decades later I found a second hand copy to replace it. She was much more classic in her taste in literature than I am; she read Proust and gave me a whole set as a wedding present — to my shame I still haven't ever read them. Ros and I were a sort of two person book group; we went on recommending books to each other to the very end of her life.

Foxglove

One almost constant presence at Christchurch Street, at least Monday to Thursday was Robin Fox, who worked with Ros. My father always called him Foxglove. Robin had been Robert's agent since the early 1950s, and was his greatest friend. Robert and Robin were in appearance and background opposites. Robin had been to Harrow and then in the war had won the MC. He was married to Angela, the illegitimate daughter of the playwright Freddie Lonsdale. They had married when they were both 21 and although the marriage had not been without its vicissitudes they were both devoted to their three sons: Edward, William (who took the stage name James) and Robert. Robin would have liked to have been an actor himself, but became a lawyer and then an agent. With his lawyer's insightful grasp of a contract, he was a very useful agent to have. Edward and James became actors, while their brother Robert is a producer. Edward and James both have children who are actors.

Just when everything seemed to be going well — Edward and James launched on their careers and Robin with his ability to court, flatter and amuse, the most powerful and respected of theatrical agents — Robin was suddenly diagnosed with lung cancer. In his desperation after a gloomy prognosis, he fell into the hands of a sadistic German charlatan who promised a cancer cure at his clinic in Switzerland. Angela wrote about this — and everything else in their lives — with her characteristic mixture of honesty and sharpness in her autobiography *Slightly Foxed by my Theatrical Family* (Collins, 1986).

By the late 1960s I had my own flat in the King's Road, just before the road twists and Chelsea becomes World's End. So I was just a stroll away from Christchurch Street and Saturday mornings were nearly always spent Chez Chatto — Sunday nights too. Saturday morning shopping started at a baker's called Beatons, which sold wonderful bread but also things like Chelsea buns and Bath buns. The rest of the shopping completed it was back to 24 Christchurch Street for coffee and a little sustenance.

One weekend Ros decided to teach Sarah Miles, Willy (James) Fox and Sarah's brother Christopher and me to make soufflés. We made cheese ones and peach ones. The twice baked soufflé is a brilliant, fail proof way of making a soufflé. At dinner parties in the '60s and '70s many people served soufflés and they were a bit of a nightmare; there was always a risk that the whole thing wouldn't rise or that it would collapse too soon. Below is my cousin Catherine's version of a twice baked cheese soufflé, the Gruyère cheese absolutely makes it and these are wonderful to have in the freezer as a little supper treat as well as to serve as an impressive start to a dinner party.

Twice baked cheese soufflé

125g butter
125g plain flour

½ teaspoon mustard
550ml milk
1 clove garlic, crushed
pinch nutmeg
8 eggs, separated
300g grated mature cheddar cheese
salt and pepper
300ml single cream
125g grated Gruyère cheese

Make a sauce by melting the butter, adding the flour and mustard and cooking a little, then whisk in the heated milk, garlic, nutmeg, salt and pepper and bring to the boil, stirring. Remove from the heat and mix in egg yolks and cheddar cheese. Season with salt and pepper. Whisk egg whites until stiff and fold in gently. Pour into 10 greased ramekins and stand these in a large roasting tin ½ full of water. Bake at 200°C for 20 minutes until they are firm. Cool, turn out and put in a large oven proof dish, a Pyrex one is ideal. Cover with foil and you can freeze them at this point.

To serve: defrost overnight in the fridge, then pour over the cream, sprinkle with the grated Gruyère and bake 15 minutes in a hot oven (200°C).

SERVES 10

Sarah Miles and Willy (James) Fox were an item. Sarah had already been cast in Joe Losey's film *The Servant* when Joe and Dirk Bogarde, who was playing the lead, saw Sarah and James together and decided to test him for a role. Of course he was perfect as the spoilt, upper class, languid young man who falls prey to the sinister man servant. James and Sarah were a stunning couple. Sarah was the sexiest person I have ever met. She was a chameleon and you never knew what she was going to come as, a gamine boyish figure in a man's shirt with her long dark curly hair pushed into a cap, or a '20s beauty in a pleated white linen skirt and a big floppy hat. She was an original; fearless, shockingly outspoken with a slightly dangerous quality, funny and the best flirt. She had not only James in thrall but any man, woman, child or dog she set out to charm. She kept the biggest dog anyone had ever seen, a Pyrenean mountain dog called Addo who accompanied her everywhere. With Addo in the Chatto's sitting room it was like negotiating one's way round a small pony.

Working life

My first job in London, organised by Ros, was working in a very grand nursery school — the school Ros's own boys had attended. One of the little boys in my class was Antony Radziwell. His mother Lee, Jackie Kennedy's sister was the only mother who ever asked if she could come and inspect the premises and "sit in" on a class. Incredibly elegant and groomed, she perched on a tiny child-sized chair and watched a session. We must have passed muster because Antony was duly enrolled.

In the summer of 1965 I became involved in a production of *Alice in Wonderland* performed in Christchurch Meadows. Sherry's Oxford contemporaries had already gone down and dispersed but the director of *Alice*, Adrian Benjamin was a friend of Nigel Frith's who had been up at Oxford with Sherry and was still around because his parents lived just outside Oxford. Adrian's production of *Alice* had multiple Alices — tall, tiny and long-necked — one of them was Tamara Ustinov, Peter Ustinov's daughter. We had live baby pigs for the baby-into-pig scene, and the White Rabbit made his entrance from miles off as he hurried along, consulting his watch. We took a cut down version of it to Rome, when I played the Dormouse and Polly Toynbee was Alice. We were chatting in the wings during one performance and Polly, slightly distracted, went on in her Alice costume and wig with a cigarette in her hand, perhaps a slightly too surreal touch even for that production.

Then Adrian asked me to play the Queen in *Richard II* which we performed at the Minack Theatre, Porthcurno, Cornwall. We all stayed on a farm, sleeping above the cows in sleeping bags and drove in Land Rovers to and from the open air theatre, built into the rocks with the sea as backdrop. Richard was played by a very good actor, Nick Loukes, but I had fallen in love with somebody else. This love affair was hopeless really because our timing was always slightly off. However, *Richard II* gave me both a desire to do more acting. Plus, I thought that if I was actually in the same city as this beautiful man with his great sense of unhappiness and unease, he might fall in love with me. When I actually moved to Oxford, just seeing him through a window could make my day. If he took me out for a drink or drove me home and we actually talked, I was in heaven. Unrequited love may be a bore but I did adore him and it was a pleasure to be sad. On the whole I have to say I had a thoroughly good time being in love.

Oxford and acting

When I decided to go and live in Oxford, a friend Tim who was working at the Oxford Playhouse suggested we might share a house or a flat. He found a flat in North Oxford, the ground floor of a Victorian villa, which he thought might suit us well. However, there was one snag — the landlady only wanted to let to girls. No problem, said Tim, he had met a girl he thought I would really like. She was an American, Barbara Schilling. He brought her to tea and I did like her and in due course we moved into the flat in Northmore Road. Barbara had been a teenage model, I had probably seen her photo in magazines like *17*. She was tall and blonde and gorgeous and soon half of Oxford was in love with her, the *Zuleika Dobson de nos jours*.

Barbara was supposed to be studying art at the Ruskin but she didn't seem to go very often. She fell in love with a charming, beautiful, kind man with a profile as perfect as hers. She eventually married him, the kind beautiful man, divorced him, moved back to America and then some years later fetched up in a Holland Park mansion as the second Mrs John Cleese.

The Bodleian Library was my place of employment; I spent my time mostly in the strange world of "the stacks", a building within a building that had no windows, and two floors of books to every one floor of the outside shell. Handle-less iron doors were opened with a key you wore on a chain round your neck. I had repeated nightmares of somehow losing the key and being locked in there. An underground railway for the books ran between the stacks and the library buildings on the opposite side of the road, and a conveyor belt brought the books up through the many levels in heavy wooden boxes which you unloaded from the outstretched arms of the conveyor belt as it clunked by. Mis-time a loading or unloading and the wooden box would slip sideways and crash down into the bowels of the conveyor belt bringing everything to a shuddering halt. An alarm would sound and men in brown Holland overalls would arrive to inspect the damage and get the whole thing going again.

For my twenty-first birthday my boss Clive said he would give me a treat; this turned out to be being shown the Bodley's collection of pornography, kept in a sort of special cage. Clive selected a few choice examples but realised quite soon it wasn't really my cup of tea. I must have a treat though, what would I prefer? Half an hour's peace deep in the stacks with old copies of *Vogue* was my choice.

Sometimes I was allowed out of the stacks and did what was called "evening duty" in the Radcliffe Camera or the incredibly beautiful Duke Humpfrey's Library. Evening duty was fun because there was usually a chum or two, and we would have a whispered conversation and usually go for a drink as soon as I was off duty.

However, my life in Oxford was mostly about acting; after *Alice* and *Richard II* I was ready for the big time. This was the Oxford University Dramatic Society's major production for the year, *Love's Labour's Lost*, directed by Frank Hauser, who ran the Oxford playhouse, where we would be performing. I had a small part, the country wench Jacquenetta — a comely slut. We had the Bristol Old Vic costumes, which were Watteau inspired, and the men in particular looked pretty as pictures in their silk and ruffles and white stockings. My costume was a blue and white striped skirt and a low, laced bodice and a big straw hat. When I came on for the dress rehearsal, Frank guffawed: "What do you think you've come as — bloody Dresden?" Luckily the wardrobe mistress, Sarah, was a chum so Frank's instructions to break everything down and dirty it all up were not taken very seriously. I made a concession to being a rustic by putting a small smudge on my cheek. Otherwise we seemed to do a modified ballet makeup, lots of black eyeliner and false eyelashes.

We took *Love's Labour's Lost* on a European tour of Caen, Paris, Grenoble, Rome and, most eccentrically, Catania in Sicily where we played in a crumbling little baroque theatre. There was not much room backstage so I would sit on a circular staircase which didn't lead anywhere and flirt with whoever else wasn't on stage at that moment. I would also do the elaborate makeup for Mercade, the messenger of death who only comes on right at the end. Ivor Roberts had prematurely white hair and in his black and silver costume with a slightly ghoulish make up, looked spectacular.

Back in Oxford I played what I always thought of as the Margaret Rutherford part in *Ring Round the Moon*. Madame Desmortes spends the play in a wheelchair which was slightly problematic as it was an outdoor production in Trinity College Gardens and the wheelchair tended to get stuck in the damp grass. I loved my part and the play, although while rehearsing and working at the Bodleian I had a sort of meltdown and couldn't stop crying. I phoned home and Robert came over to Oxford and took me out for dinner. In my diary I wrote of playing the part: "God, I am scared of it. Real deep down afraid."

Every time I thought I had moved on, the object of my unrequited affection would hover into sight again usually at a party. Eventually, though, our lives and our circles of friends diverged and he became a "former attachment". As Robert Frost wrote in a poem called just that:

"You know the ship is moving when you see

The boxes on the quayside slide away

And become smaller — and feel a calm delight

When the port's cleared and the coast out of sight

And ships are few, each on its proper course

With no occasion for approach or discourse."

Of course, I had yet to find what my proper course was.

Even being in a rather strange comedy about multiple births at the Edinburgh festival didn't really dampen my enthusiasm to act. It took a few weeks in rep at Palmers Green in a truly terrible production of *Gaslight* and a lot of nerve wracking auditions for parts I didn't get for me to decide I couldn't spend my life doing this.

(No) red shoes

In a letter to my mother before they married, Robert wrote that his friend Peter Bull was in love with "a girl who is in Portugal —

I suppose we all have our problems." This girl was the wonderful Mary Cook. By the time I met her she was running a domestic employment agency called Solve Your Problem (SYP). She had been married to a Portuguese nobleman, the Count Seruya (known as Foxy) and had lived in Lisbon before returning to London during the war to nurse her mother. It seems she never returned to Foxy. In 1944 she had become head of entertainment for the Nuffield Centre, then operating out of the disused Café de Paris and she "discovered" Peter Sellers, Harry Secombe, Benny Hill, Tommy Cooper, Tony Hancock, Michael Bentine, Frankie Howard and Ronnie Corbett.

From an office on the first floor of a building on a corner of Kensington Church Street, Mary Cook interviewed would-be housekeepers, cooks, nannies and mother's helps. SYP advertised in *The Lady* and prospective employers would phone in their requests and a matching process would (hopefully) take place. Employees' details were entered on an index file. When I went to work at SYP in the early 1970s I realised that, like me, many people were adept at reading upside down and so we adopted a code to prevent applicants from reading their own files during interview. "NBG" meant No Bloody Good, "NBD–pending?" meant the person seemed on the edge of a nervous breakdown and "IF" stood for Invisible Friends — or really dotty. Mary also had the wonderfully descriptive phrase "Will his/her opinion of him/herself be shared by others?" which meant someone was "up themselves" as we would say less elegantly today.

Before I worked in the office I did jobs through SYP. In the late '60s I ·· sent to see a Mrs Gowing who lived in a flat in Percy Street, off the Tottenham Court Road. When she opened the front door of the flat, which was up a narrow staircase, her first words were "Oh, you're a blonde, my husband ran off with a blonde." Mrs Gowing was Julia Strachey, a niece of Lytton's and thus intimately connected to the Bloomsbury group: the Woolfs, Vanessa and Clive Bell,

Duncan Grant, David Garnett and the writer and diarist Frances Partridge. Written in pencil on the wall above the telephone at Mrs Gowing's flat were the words: "Best Friend: Frances Partridge" and a telephone number. Mrs Partridge, the last survivor of that fascinating and intimately connected group, wrote a biography of her friend, *Julia*, which captures her contradictory and sometimes infuriating personality but is suffused with her endearing eccentricity, sharp wit and facility with words.

Like Mary Lennox in *The Secret Garden*, Julia was a child of the Raj, sent away from India and her parents at a very young age, to go to school in England. Frances and Julia met at Bedales and became best friends. In the holidays Julia stayed with various relations, mainly with her Quaker aunt, Aunty Loo and *her* brother, the writer and essayist Logan Pearsall Smith. Some summers she spent at I Tatti, Bernard Berenson's villa outside Florence where she wandered the corridors in the early mornings gazing at the exquisite paintings of saints being martyred in particularly horrible ways. As a young woman she modelled for Patou in Paris. She was tall and thin with red hair, fashionably Eton-cropped, white skin and slanting green cat's eyes. She was taken up by her Uncle Lytton's friends, particularly (Dora) Carrington, the painter who fell in love with Lytton and lived with him for the rest of his life, committing suicide after his death. Encouraged by Lytton and Carrington she wrote a novel, *Cheerful Weather for the Wedding* which was published by the Hogarth Press in 1932 and, also with the encouragement of Lytton and Carrington, she married the sculptor Stephen Tomlin, known always as Tommy. Tommy was bi-sexual and prone to depression.

The Bloomsbury mores encouraged a freewheeling attitude to sex and Mrs G would tell me about going to parties with Tommy where he would, as she put it "set his cap at someone" and have to have them, more or less there and then. "Just another scalp for his belt" as she said. Not surprisingly the marriage came unstuck and at the beginning of the war Julia fell in love with, and later married, Laurence Gowing, who was considerably younger than she was (he was 21 at the time they met) and whom she mothered and protected. She moved with him to live in Newcastle and later Leeds. Not all that long before I went to work for her, he had left her for a younger woman who became his second wife, Jenny Wallis. Mrs G continued to spend Christmases and weekends with them and the three daughters they eventually produced.

The flat in Percy Street had a large living room whose floor sloped, so that a pencil dropped in one corner rolled across to the opposite corner. There was a green Casa Pupo rug, some wonderful small sculptures by Tomlin, one was of Europa and the Bull and an unfinished oil by Carrington of cows in a field. She also had some of Carrington's foil under glass works which were extraordinarily decorative and witty. Mrs G was endlessly writing and rewriting her memoirs as well as fragments of a novel about Carrington. Some days we would sit on her bed surrounded by the illustrated letters Carrington had sent her, endlessly sorting and re-sorting. I realised quite early on that she needed someone to talk to as much as she needed a secretary — and I was a hopeless secretary anyway. In those days if you made a mistake, the whole page or letter had to be retyped, I don't think even Tippex existed. One day Mrs G asked me to stay for lunch and produced one of the most eccentric meals I have ever been offered. It was a watercress salad (just watercress) and a bar of Cadbury's Dairy Milk Chocolate. She drank Chivas Regal, while I drank water. "A perfectly balanced meal," Mrs G said proudly. When she discovered I could cook, my hours and my role changed, I would stay to cook and eat lunch with her.

The only things she had published since the early 1930s was a novel *The Man on The Pier* and a short story for *The New Yorker*, called *Can't You Get Me Out Of Here*, a surreal fantasy about an insect who has fallen into a bowl of spaghetti. When she died, Frances Partridge attempted to create some order from the chaos of files, notebooks and diaries I had faced when I first walked up the rickety stairs to the Percy Street flat. Mrs Partridge wove these into *Julia, A portrait of Julia Strachey by Herself and Frances Partridge*. Some days when the intake of whisky and purple hearts had exacerbated Mrs G's sense that the world was a nightmarish, cruel place, I wondered if I wasn't going a bit mad too.

After a happy stint working in a secondhand and antiquarian bookshop in the Earl's Court Road, Mary Cook asked me to come and work in the office of SYP. This was always very congenial; there was always at least one other "girl" besides Mary and me. Mary's eccentric cousin would call in sometimes. It was he who bankrolled the company and he would come to inspect the books; he was just known as "Cousin", a little dapper, slightly effete man who wore his hanky tucked into his jacket sleeve. At Christmas we got a nice cash bonus as a thank you for the year's work. In subsequent places of employment I have always been amazed that more employers don't do this: just when you need it at that costly time of year there you are with a few pounds or dollars you weren't expecting. I now realise too that when the people running the business work alongside their employees they have a much better grasp of what makes people happy or unhappy in their jobs.

While I was working at SYP, two clients, Princess Alice of Gloucester and Lady Churchill phoned asking for a parlourmaid. Princess Alice actually got some wretched lady-in-waiting to make the call, but the wonderful Clemmie phoned in person. Neither of them could get their heads around the fact that there was no one who wanted to be a parlourmaid by 1968. All I could do to placate them was to promise faithfully that the next person to walk through the door with parlourmaid experience and references would be dispatched to one of them immediately.

Mary also had her quirks, one of which was that she wouldn't put anyone on the books if they came for an interview with us wearing red shoes. Red shoes equalled "tart" in her book and she couldn't be swayed from this belief. A charming and beautiful girl came in one day; she was ideal mother's help material and as soon as she'd gone I went whiffling through my book to see where I could send her. Mary stopped me, the girl couldn't be sent anywhere because she had been wearing red espadrilles.

In quiet moments I would make Mary tell me the stories of her life in Lisbon. One anecdote I never tired of hearing was about a very grand party where the wife of the American ambassador had made a lemon meringue pie, her speciality. There was no room for it in the kitchen so Mary had the brilliant idea of putting it in the bathroom, where she carefully balanced it on top of the bidet. Unfortunately the ambassador's wife went to wash her hands and was mortally offended at the location of her masterpiece.

Tarte au citron

PÂTÉ SABLE OR SHORT CRUST PASTRY
    140g butter
    250g plain flour, sifted
    30g ground almonds
    100g icing sugar
    1 egg
    pinch of salt
FILLING
    4 lemons
    9 eggs
    375g sugar
    300ml double cream

Make the pastry by rubbing the cold, cubed butter into the flour, adding the almonds and icing sugar and enough very cold water to bind the pastry. Or make pastry in a food mixer.

Line a flan or tart tin and refrigerate, then bake blind for 15 minutes at 180°C. Cool.

Grate lemons then squeeze them. Beat the eggs with the sugar. Whisk cream until slightly thickened, stir juice and rind into eggs and sugar mix, fold in cream. Fill tart case. Bake at 180°C for about 45 minutes or until just set. Serve covered in sifted icing sugar. Don't refrigerate.

SERVES 6–8

Through SYP I went to do some secretarial work for Rebecca West in a dark flat somewhere in Kensington. All the furniture had clawed feet and Rebecca West lay in bed with an eye patch, having had a cataract operation. It was probably just as well she couldn't clearly see the letters I typed, badly. I can't think now why I was so resistant to learning to type properly. In those days if you didn't do a Constance Spry cookery course when you left school, you did a secretarial course. I suppose I always thought I could sort of bluff my way through.

One summer I worked for Joe Losey, the film director. He was a client of Ros's and when his secretary Celia went on holiday, Ros suggested I take her place. Joe and Patricia his wife lived in Royal Avenue, Chelsea in the house where *The Servant* was filmed. Joe's office was right at the top of the house and I would let myself in and climb up to the office and, once the magic hour of ten o'clock had passed, put any phone calls through to Joe. One morning about 9.15 the phone rang. It was an old acquaintance of Joe's called Baroness Budberg. Moura Budberg was a White Russian who had been the mistress of both Gorky and HG Wells but now hung around the fringes of the film world hitching her wagon to anyone of use. She reminded me of an old toad but this morning her ringing imperative demanded I put Joe on the line. I buzzed Joe and a cross sleepy growl answered. "Baroness Budberg for you, Joe" I said quickly, putting her through. The line was busy for a while, then Joe hung up and a few minutes later came up the stairs, in his dressing gown, furious: "I thought I told you never to put a call through before ten!" "You did, Joe," I replied. "But it was a question of who I was more scared of, Moura Budberg or you, and she won."

Joe, used to an efficient secretary who could touch type, take dictation and get whomever he wanted on the phone at a moment's notice, just gave up the unequal struggle, taught me to make him bullshots (vodka and frozen consommé) which he sometimes started drinking about 11.30 in the morning. After a couple of those, he would take me out to lunch at an Italian restaurant in the King's Road.

When I was between jobs and at a loose end, which was quite often, I was ready to go anywhere. This was why Robert's suggestion that we go to Australia in 1973 was so seductive. In Australia I could be an unknown quantity, I could re-invent myself.

MARY COOK AT "FAIRMANS"

Cover of UK *Good Housekeeping*, Christmas Edition (1953)

Chapter Twelve

TWO CHRISTMASES

Christmas at "Fairmans" always meant my father precariously perched on a step-ladder, knocking drawing pins into the beams in the sitting-room ceiling so the Christmas cards could be displayed. It was always a worry that there wouldn't be enough cards to cover the beams but there were always enough cards to cover the beams and even to put along above the pelmets of the curtains. Christmas cards from people who sent photographs of themselves, like Mr and Mrs Yehudi Menuhin (she was always inexplicably wearing a dirndl) were displayed on the mantelpiece. The Red Cross sent a photograph of Her Majesty, their patron, and Robert liked people to think it was from Her Majesty Herself — just for a tease. He usually displayed it bent back so the Red Cross logo couldn't be seen. Nancy Mitford often sent a photo of herself: "from the French lady writer."

Robert loved decorations so he would go somewhere in Soho in about September and buy garlands of tinsel and gaudy Christmas tree decorations. If he had been to Hong Kong or New York recently, the decorations were even better. There were some wonderful bubbling Christmas tree lights which had been bought in New York in the 1950s and needed a special transformer. There was always a real Christmas tree, selected by Joan from the nursery on the lower road into Henley, just before the bridge. A bunch of mistletoe hung in the hall, my mother fussing because the berries dropped and then were trodden on and squashed into the hall rug.

Sometime before Christmas Eve the bell ringers would arrive, village worthies who had walked the mile or so from Wargrave. They arranged their handbells on the dining room table and then rang out Christmas carols. After each one, their leader would say "Any special requests Mr Morley?" and my tone-deaf father would say "What about Good King Wenceslas?" to which the answer was inevitably, "We just played that one."

Robert liked everything about Christmas except doing up the presents. He always lost the end of the Sellotape when wrapping the bottles of whisky he bought as presents for people like Mr Gilkes the garage owner, Alfred the barber, and Lucy the doctors' receptionist, who Robert believed — with some justification — was a better diagnostician than either of the doctors.

Apart from the whisky, Robert was a generous and sometimes inspired present-giver. Joan usually got jewellery or clothes from him. She was not an easy person to give presents to. "Oh, lovely darling," she would say, on a dying fall as she opened the jewel box or lifted the lid on the dress or coat he had picked out. He would immediately reply "I've got the receipt." Coats were safer than dresses and a brooch, particularly of an animal, a donkey, an owl, rabbit or cat, was often a success.

The presents were placed in piles under the Christmas tree to be undone in as short a time as possible — except, of course, by Joan because she spent Christmas morning in the kitchen, cooking lunch. Only after lunch had been eaten, every dish and glass washed up and put away, could she be persuaded to come and sit down and open her presents. Then later there would be the obligatory search through the dustbin for some present or part of a present that had been inadvertently thrown away with the wrapping paper.

When I say that my mother cooked Christmas lunch, that was true, except that everything had been prepared for her by Mrs Haycock, the cook or Mrs Silver, who succeeded Mrs Haycock. Mrs Haycock looked like an idealised "Mrs Bun the Baker's Wife" in the Happy Families card game. She was short and rather rotund with white hair and pink cheeks. She would leave the vegetables for Christmas lunch peeled and standing in bowls of cold water in the larder, with a slice of lemon to stop the potatoes blackening. Every sprout would be marked with a cross on its stalk end. The turkey would be stuffed and in the fridge, sausage meat one end, chestnuts the other. The Christmas pudding, at least a year old, would be in a pudding basin, tied up in a linen cloth and ready to be steamed on top of the Aga. Bread sauce and brandy butter were in the fridge.

The Christmas Day staples: turkey, ham and pudding

In Sydney these days we have developed our own Christmas traditions and the starter is always prawns and oysters. Then we continue with turkey and ham.

I used to be nervous of cooking a whole turkey — and let's face it, it is not the most interesting of birds — but this turkey breast recipe is good with its proportion of fruity stuffing to rather bland meat.

Roast turkey with sausage, apple and cranberry stuffing

(adapted from UK *Good Housekeeping*, November 2002)

50g butter
1 onion, chopped
2 cloves garlic, crushed
75g dried cranberries
2 tbs chopped parsley
4 good pork sausages, skinned and broken up
2 red eating apples
2kg turkey breast (frozen is fine)
3 tbs olive oil
4–5 bay leaves

Preheat oven to 200°C (180°C if fan-forced). Put two or three wooden skewers to soak in cold water.

For the stuffing: melt the butter in a frying pan, add onion and sauté for 5 minutes or until soft. Add garlic and cook a further minute. Tip into a bowl and allow to cool slightly. Add cranberries, parsley and sausage meat. Core and chop one of the apples and add to mixture. Season well with salt and pepper. Put the turkey joint on a board. Skin side down and cut along the middle of the joint to just over ¾ of the way through. Season then add the stuffing and put joint back into shape. Secure with skewers and, if necessary, twine or string.

Calculate cooking time at 20 minutes per 450g plus 20 minutes. Put in a roasting tin, drizzle with olive oil and cover with foil. Slice the remaining apple into rounds. Remove foil 30 minutes before end and place apple slices and bay leaves on the joint. Roast uncovered for the final 30 minutes.

SERVES 6

Here's an Italian take on the turkey.

Lombardy turkey

>6kg whole turkey
>125g butter
>2 sprigs rosemary
>½ bunch sage

GRAVY
>125ml chicken stock
>splash white wine
>marsala

STUFFING
>2 onions, chopped
>3 cloves garlic, crushed
>6 slices pancetta, chopped or 3 rashers of bacon, chopped
>¼ cup olive oil
>300g ciabatta breadcrumbs
>⅓ cup toasted pine nuts
>⅓ cup chopped flat leaf parsley
>1 tbs chopped rosemary leaves
>finely grated zest of a lemon
>4 tbs grated parmesan
>½ cup chicken stock
>4 crumbled and skinned Tuscan style sausages with fennel seeds

For the stuffing, cook onions, garlic and pancetta in the oil for 10 minutes then add herbs, crumbs, pine nuts and lemon zest and fry. Add stock gradually, you want it moist but not soggy. Cool stuffing and then stuff turkey with the Tuscan sausages for the neck end cavity.

Preheat oven to 180°C. Place turkey in roasting tin and cover the breast with butter. Add sage leaves and sprigs of rosemary. Season with salt and pepper. Cover the whole pan with baking paper and then a layer of foil. Roast for 20 minutes per 500g.

Make the gravy with pan juices, chicken stock and white wine. Add a dash of marsala.

I serve this with hot vegetables and roast potatoes if it's a cool day or salads if it's hot: usually a green salad, a tomato salad, or perhaps that mixture of watermelon, fetta, mint and black olives and always a potato salad.

POTATO SALAD
- 1kg chat potatoes
- 2–3 tbsp mayonnaise or yoghurt
- 2 tbs French dressing
- 4–5 spring onions or 1 red onion
- ½ cup chives, chopped
- 2 tbs dill, chopped
- 2 tbs mint, chopped
- 3-4 rashers bacon, crumbled and fried

Make the potato salad and dress it while it's hot with either a mixture of half mayonnaise and French dressing or some yoghurt, then add spring onions, finely chopped and/or red onion, chives and dill, or perhaps mint. Crumbled fried bacon is a nice addition.

SERVES 10–12

At Christmas a ham is a wonderful thing. I buy one with a Polish brand from my local deli in Bondi Junction. It feeds our Christmas party guests served with small soft white rolls and butter. People can make themselves a ham roll and add chutney or mustard.

To glaze the ham make a mixture of orange and pineapple juice, add brown sugar and mustard and simmer until you have a nice thick glaze. Skin the ham, stud the fat with cloves and brush over the glaze. Cook for about 30–40 minutes in a hot oven, basting frequently with the glaze.

Here's a recipe for using up leftover ham.

Cold parsleyed ham

1kg ham
500ml chicken or veal stock
150ml white wine
black pepper and nutmeg
6–8 tbs chopped parsley
2 tbs powdered gelatine
1–2 tbs tarragon vinegar

Carve the ham off in chunks and dice.

Simmer the diced ham gently in the stock and white wine for 5 minutes. Season with pepper and nutmeg. Drain, reserving the stock and place diced ham in a wet glass bowl or terrine dish, dusted with some of the chopped parsley. Soften the gelatine in a little hot water and stir into stock with vinegar and parsley. Allow to cool and become syrupy and then pour over the ham. There should be enough liquid to cover the ham. Allow to set in fridge overnight. Unmould if you are feeling brave or just serve from the dish.

SERVES 6

Now the Christmas pudding, this one is quite innovative in that it's cooked in the oven in a bain-marie.

Christmas pudding

>   800g mixed dried fruit
>   finely grated rind and juice of 1 orange
>   150ml brandy, Cointreau or Grand Marnier
>   3 tbs black treacle
>   1 large Granny Smith apple, grated
>   50g white breadcrumbs
>   50g plain flour
>   1 tbs mixed spice
>   100g blanched chopped almonds
>   2 large eggs, beaten
>   125g butter well chilled

Put mixed dried fruit, orange zest and juice, brandy and treacle into a large mixing bowl, cover and leave for a couple of hours or overnight at room temperature. Preheat oven to 180°C. Grease a 1.8-litre pudding basin and line with a circle of baking paper. Add apple to soaked fruit along with breadcrumbs, flour, spice, almonds and eggs, then grate over butter. Stir well. (The butter tends to stick in clumps but don't worry.) Spoon mixture into pudding basin, level the top and cover with two thicknesses of baking paper and then a layer of foil. Make sure the foil is secured around the edge of the basin. Stand the basin in a deep roasting pan (one with handles is good). Pour boiling water into the tin to come about halfway up the sides of the pudding basin. Now cover the whole pan with a large piece of foil and secure the edges. Carefully transfer the whole thing to the oven and cook for 6 hours at 180°C. Have a look into the pan to check it's not boiling dry.

When it's cool you can take the pudding out and freeze it.

To reheat on Christmas day, cook in the bain-marie for about an hour.

SERVES 8–10

This Christmas pudding is adapted from a Maggie Beer recipe. I use candied lemon peel instead of citron peel. I also finish off the recipe by steaming it on Christmas Day.

I make my brandy butter with cumquat brandy. Combine equal amounts of butter and sugar (half icing, half brown) with brandy to taste.

Christmas pudding II

   120g chopped citron or lemon peel
   250g mixed peel
   250g dried currants, seedless raisins and sultanas
   300ml tawny port
   80g (1 cup) flaked almonds
   ¾ cup plain flour
   pinch each of cinnamon, nutmeg, ginger and mace
   1 tsp salt
   225g cold butter
   225g (3¼ cups) stale breadcrumbs
   3 eggs, whisked

Combine fruit, port and almonds in a large glass or china bowl, mix. Cover with plastic wrap and leave at room temperature for 24 hours. Sift flour, spices and salt into a large bowl and grate in the butter, use the coarsest part of the grater. Stir in breadcrumbs and fruit and then eggs and mix well. Spoon mixture into pudding basin, level the top and cover with two thicknesses of baking paper and then a layer of foil.

Make sure the foil is secured around the edge of the basin. Stand the basin in a deep roasting pan (one with handles is good). Pour boiling water into the tin to come about halfway up the sides of the pudding basin. Now cover the whole pan with a large piece of foil and secure the edges. Carefully transfer the whole thing to the oven and cook for 6 hours at 180°C. Have a look into the pan to check it's not boiling dry.

When it's cool you can take the pudding out and freeze it.

Reheat by steaming for 1 hour on Christmas Day.

SERVES 16

After Christmas lunch and an orgy of unwrapping presents it was usually time to go to G's house on the banks of the River Thames at Henley for Christmas tea.

As G's birthday was on December 18th, she would recycle, where possible, gifts she had been given and re-gift them as Christmas presents. One year Sherry and his wife Margaret, who were living in a fireplace-less Paddington flat, were rather cast down to be given a large unwrapped log basket, albeit decoratively filled with shredded cellophane in various colours. As Sherry idly turfed out the cellophane all manner of goodies were revealed: a side of smoked salmon, a tin of pâté de foie gras, exotic teas and packets of biscuits, a jar of Fortnum and Mason honey, cheeses, Blue Mountain coffee, bottles of wine. G hadn't realised there was anything in the log basket so her face was a picture, torn as she was between wanting to claim the loot but having to admit to the re-gifting. In the end she said nothing, just accepted thanks for the treasures through gritted teeth. What made it all the funnier was that G and Margaret didn't care much for each other. On the way home in the car a philosophical discussion took place on the moral duty of Sherry and Margaret to accept the log basket but return the loot. I sided with them in their determination to hang onto the consumables as well as the (useless to them) log basket.

I'm not suggesting anyone wants to eat Christmas cake on Christmas day but a Christmas cake is definitely part of the tradition. This one is not the traditional dark fruit cake but a lighter one, as pretty as a stained glass window when cut. You can ice it with a layer of marzipan, just roll it out very thinly. I usually also cover the cake with a layer of bought royal icing.

Glacé Christmas cake

> 225g dried apricots
> 75ml brandy or sherry
> 225g glacé cherries
> 50g crystallised orange peel
> 150g glacé pineapple
> 125g walnuts
> 125g sultanas
> 225g butter
> 225g castor sugar
> 2 lemons, zest and juice
> 25g ground almonds
> 4 large eggs, beaten
> 225g plain flour, sifted
> a pinch of salt
> apricot jam to glaze
> packet of almond paste (marzipan)
> packet of fondant icing

Coarsely chop apricots (scissors are best) and soak in the alcohol 2 hours or overnight. Chop glacé fruit, cherries and walnuts. Line a tin, a square 20cm one is ideal. Beat butter and sugar with grated lemon peel. Beat in almonds, eggs. Fold in sifted flour and salt alternately with 4 tablespoons of lemon juice and then the fruit and alcohol. Add more alcohol if needed to produce a soft consistency. Bake at 170°C for 1½ hours. Reduce heat to 130°C and bake a further 2 hours or until a skewer comes out clean. Cover with foil if browning too much.

When cool brush with melted apricot jam and cover with almond paste, then brush with jam again and cover with the fondant icing.

MAKES A LARGE CAKE

Certosino

This is adapted from a Nigella recipe which she got from Anna del Conte and changed — adding more apple and taking out the candied peel. I have further changed it by removing the fennel seeds which I find overpowering and adding some candied orange peel. It is a delicious cake, a little reminiscent of panforte with its mixture of chocolate, spice and nuts. It looks stunning decorated with a mixture of glacé fruit, pecan nuts, whole almonds and cherries. Brush the cooled cake with apricot jam, heated and sieved, then arrange the fruit and nuts; brush again to glaze.

>   75g seedless raisins
>   30ml dry marsala
>   2⅓ cups plain flour
>   2 tsp bicarbonate of soda
>   150g runny honey
>   150g castor sugar
>   40g butter
>   1 tsp ground cinnamon
>   2 apples coarsely grated

200g blanched almonds, coarsely chopped
50g pine nuts
50g candied orange peel
50g glacé orange peel
75g dark chocolate, chopped
75g walnuts, chopped

Preheat oven to 180°C. Line a 22cm springform pan with baking paper. Soak raisins in marsala for 20mins. Measure flour and soda into a large bowl. Heat honey, sugar and butter with 3 tablespoons of water in a saucepan until the sugar dissolves. Add cinnamon and candied peels. Pour mixture into flour and stir to combine. Mix in all the other ingredients, the raisins and their liquid and combine well. Spoon into the tin and bake for ¾–1 hour. Cover the tin with foil for the last 15 minutes.

SERVES 8–10

Here is a very quick and good standby, a boiled fruit cake. It seems to me a very Australian thing — I can imagine some beleaguered country woman making this in 40 degree heat. At least it's quick to make but you must let the boiled mixture cool before you add the other ingredients.

Boiled fruit cake

1 cup of water
125g butter
375g mixed dried fruit
1 packet glacé cherries
1 cup sugar
1 tsp bicarbonate of soda

1 tsp mixed spice
pinch of salt
1 cup plain flour
1 cup self raising flour
2 eggs, beaten

Boil water, butter, fruit, sugar, soda, salt and mixed spice in a saucepan for 10 minutes. Cool. Add sifted flours and eggs. Mix well. Bake in a cake tin lined with baking paper at 160°C for 1¼–1½ hours. Test with skewer. Leave to cool 15 minutes before turning out.

SERVES 8–10

Christmas parties

Christmas is about parties and so we always have one. The tree must be up and decorated but don't leave it too late in December. Try not to have the party on Christmas Eve or you will feel you have only just washed up the last dirty glass and retired to bed when it's time to get up with a thumping hangover and calculate the turkey cooking time.

Here are my party staples:
- a whole ham, with soft white bread rolls, a slab of butter and a couple of chutneys. Let people make their own ham rolls.
- a whole brie, surrounded by cherries.
- a platter of crudités: carrot sticks, celery and cucumber, raw cauliflower and radishes — buy or make hummus and guacamole.

Smoked salmon pancakes

120g plain flour
2 large eggs
180ml milk
2 dessertspoons butter, melted
2 tbsp light cream cheese
2 tbsp crème fraiche
1 tbs lemon juice
2 tsp horseradish
200g smoked salmon
black pepper
tbsp each dill and chives

Make the thinnest pancakes you can. You will get between 8 and 12 pancakes depending on the size of your pan.

Add the liquid slowly to the flour and beat until the batter is covered with bubbles. Let the batter stand in a cool place for an hour or two and then stir in melted butter. Heat a large non-stick frying pan and melt a knob of butter in it, then cook the pancakes.

When the pancakes are made, lay two out slightly overlapping at one end. Spread with a mixture of light cream cheese and crème fraiche into which you have added lemon juice and horseradish. Lay slices of smoked salmon over the cream cheese mixture, grind over black pepper and sprinkle with dill and chives. Roll the pancakes up tightly, wrap in cling film.

When ready to serve slice into rounds and stand on their ends like sushi.

MAKES ABOUT 30 ROLLS

Another good party staple are onion and goats' cheese tartlets.

Caramelised onion and goats' cheese tartlets

> 20g butter
> 1 tbs olive oil
> 2 large white onions, finely chopped
> 1 clove garlic
> 1 tbsp sugar
> 3 eggs, beaten
> 2 tbsp cream
> salt and pepper
> 1 "log" of goats' cheese
> fresh thyme, chopped
>
> SHORTCRUST PASTRY
> 250g plain flour
> 125g cold butter
> pinch of salt

Put flour and chopped butter and salt in a food processor and whizz until the mixture resembles breadcrumbs, then add enough cold water to bind pastry. Fill small tartlet cases.

Melt butter and olive oil. Fry onions until soft with garlic. Cook until soft and then sprinkle with sugar. Cover the pan with foil and cook until brown and caramelised. Add this to eggs beaten with cream, salt and pepper. Fill the tartlet cases with mixture. Crumble over a "log" of goats' cheese and sprinkle with thyme. Bake in the usual way.

If you can serve them warm, they are more delicious.

Presents

I started making these truffles as Christmas presents when I was still in my teens. Keep them in the fridge. I like them flavoured with Bacardi rum but you can use brandy or whisky.

French truffles

> 120g plain dark chocolate
> 60g butter
> 2 egg yolks
> 90g icing sugar, sieved
> 2 tsp rum
> cocoa, sieved

Melt chocolate and butter over hot water, blend in egg yolks and icing sugar, flavour with rum. Refrigerate and, when a suitable consistency, roll into balls and cover in sieved cocoa.

MAKES 15–20

These spiced peaches are really to serve with cold meats or terrines but I have successfully served them with vanilla ice cream as a pudding. In Australia stone fruits come into season just before Christmas. These peaches, or you could use nectarines, look very pretty in their jars.

Spiced peaches

> 5 medium-sized ripe peaches, peeled, stoned and quartered
> SYRUP
> 4 level tbs granulated sugar

200ml water
100ml white wine
3 tbs white wine vinegar
1 stick cinnamon, broken up
2 cloves
2 star anise
6 peppercorns, crushed

Put syrup ingredients into a medium-sized saucepan and stir over low heat until the sugar has dissolved, then bring to the boil and simmer for 2 minutes. Add the peaches and bring the syrup back to the boil. Cover with a lid and cook over low heat for 10 minutes or until peaches are tender but still hold their shape. Lift the peaches out and simmer the liquid until syrup and reduced to about 150ml. Cool the syrup slightly then pack peaches into sterilised jars and pour the liquid over. Seal the jars and allow to cool.

MAKES 3 SMALL JARS

If you have children visiting over the Christmas season, make these little stars and put them into cellophane bags as a little gift.

Spiced Christmas stars

250g softened butter
¾ cup soft brown sugar
1 tsp grated orange rind
1 tsp vanilla extract
2½ cups plain flour, sifted
1 tsp ground ginger
½ tsp ground cinnamon
pinch of salt

Beat butter, sugar, orange rind and vanilla until light and fluffy. Sift over flour, spices and salt. Mix with a knife until a dough forms, adding a little water if needed. Cover with cling film and refrigerate 30 minutes. Divide dough into two pieces and roll out between two sheets of baking paper. Use star-shaped cutters to cut out dough. Transfer biscuits to greased baking sheets and bake at 160°C for 15–20 minutes.

These stars can be iced when they are cool with a glacé icing made with lemon juice and icing sugar.

MAKES 30–40 STARS

Sydney Christmases

My first experience of Sydney was in 1949 when Robert brought his play *Edward My Son* to Sydney following a season on Broadway. The central character in *Edward* is Arnold Holt, a corrupt businessman who is prepared to lie, cheat, bully and blackmail to get his own way and increase his fortune. In the process he drives his wife to drink, loses his beloved only son and at the end of the play is about to continue the pattern by taking over his grandson's upbringing. Robert had no intention of playing the lead character himself but actor after actor rejected the part as being deeply unsympathetic. And so he is, but Robert gave him wit and charm. When Holt appeals directly to the audience they become complicit in his deals and schemes. The play looked to the future, to a rising generation of wheeler-dealer business moguls out to make a killing from the debris and destruction at the end of World War II.

My mother was not very impressed with Sydney at the end of the 1940s. We rented a house in what is now one of Sydney's most expensive neighbourhoods, Wolseley Road, Point Piper. Robert gave a spectacular fireworks party. A local Italian restaurant catered and my mother's lasting memory of the evening was seeing Morty Gottleib, the company manager, running from his car to the house in a thunderstorm carrying two galvanised iron buckets full of zabaglione, as huge raindrops splashed around him.

My first impressions of Sydney, I can hardly count 1949, were thoroughly positive when I came back with Robert in 1973. Again, a play was our meal ticket; this time Alan Ayckbourn's *How the Other Half Loves*.

After nearly 30 years of living here Christmas still takes me by surprise, one minute the jacarandas are in bloom and the next it's time to order the ham. I still do the traditional things for Christmas, the turkey, the ham and the pudding but besides the entertaining there are always those hot nights when you just want to flop about, put on a DVD and eat something simple.

Cold soups are fresh and summery: for years and years I made this one, after I did a Cordon Bleu course in the 1960s. At the end of every class the students got to take home what had been cooked. We drew lots for the food and I won this soup, gallons of it. London was having one of its heatwaves and I lived on cold soup for days.

Lebanese cucumber soup

150ml chicken stock
150ml tomato juice
150ml single cream
500g yoghurt
1 clove garlic
1 large telegraph cucumber, peeled and diced
1 cup shelled prawns
1 tablespoon chopped mint
1 hardboiled egg, chopped

Mix stock, tomato juice, cream and yoghurt. Add garlic, cucumber and prawns and season well. Chill, serve garnished with mint and hardboiled egg.

SERVES 4

Another cold soup I have been making for many years is green pea soup.

Green pea soup

> 1 onion, chopped
> half a lettuce, shredded
> 500g frozen petit pois
> 1L chicken stock
> salt and pepper
> pinch of sugar

Sweat the chopped onion and lettuce in a good knob of butter, add frozen peas and chicken stock to cover. Season with salt and pepper and add sugar. Simmer until the onion is soft and then blend and chill, add a swirl of cream and some chopped herbs (mint or chives or both) when serving.

SERVES 4

Here is a very elegant soup, you can garnish it with prawns or crabmeat. I like it with just a sprinkling of chopped chives.

Buttermilk vichyssoise

> 110g butter
> 4 large or 6 mediums leeks, well washed and sliced finely
> 200g potatoes, peeled and chopped

2 medium onions, finely chopped
500ml chicken stock
salt and pepper
500ml buttermilk
100ml milk
salt and pepper

Melt the butter in a large saucepan and add leeks, potatoes and onions. Cover and cook gently for 20 minutes, checking that vegetables are softening but not colouring. Add chicken stock, season with salt and pepper and cook for 10 minutes or until potato is soft. Cool. Blend with milk and buttermilk and add more stock if you find it is too thick. Chill.

SERVES 6

Salmorejo is a cousin of gazpacho. This recipe comes from my friend, Valerie Levy, and tastes of the very essence of tomato.

Salmorejo

100g stale, crustless bread
4 cloves crushed garlic
salt and pepper
1kg ripe tomatoes, peeled and chopped
¼ cup cider vinegar
¾ cup extra virgin olive oil
200ml tomato juice

Soak bread in water and squeeze dry. Put in a blender with garlic, salt, pepper, tomatoes and vinegar. Blend. Add olive oil a little at a time. Thin with tomato juice. Chill.

Garnish with (or serve in little bowls alongside the soup) finely-chopped parsley, chopped ham and hardboiled egg.

SERVES 4

Sometimes a warm starter is a good idea; this can be a starter or a nice lunch dish. It's a version of pizzaladiere, itself the Niçoise version of pizza.

Tomato pissaladiere

PASTRY DOUGH
- 2 cups plain flour
- pinch of salt
- 125g cold butter, cut into small pieces
- 2 large eggs, beaten

TOPPING
- 1 small onion finely chopped
- 2 cloves garlic, crushed
- 1 small zucchini, diced
- 1kg medium ripe tomatoes, sliced
- 250g cherry tomatoes
- 85g anchovy fillets
- grated parmesan cheese
- basil
- olive oil

To sifted flour, add salt and butter and process in a food processor until mixture is like breadcrumbs. Add beaten eggs and process until mixture forms a ball. Wrap in cling film and refrigerate for 30 minutes. Line a quiche tin or a square baking sheet with the rolled out pastry.

Cook onion and garlic in olive oil until soft. Add zucchini and cook until starting to soften. Season and allow to cool a little, then spread over pastry base. Cover with the sliced tomatoes, filling in gaps with the halved cherry tomatoes. Arrange anchovy fillets on top, sprinkle with chopped basil and grated parmesan. Drizzle with olive oil and cook at 190°C on a high shelf for 25 minutes then reduce heat to 160°C and bake a further 20–25 minutes. Make sure base is cooked under the topping.

Serve warm with salad leaves.

SERVES 6

Something I have been making for many years is Coronation chicken. Constance Spry made this dish for the Queen's Coronation in 1952. (Constance Spry, as well as being famous for her flower arrangement skills, ran a finishing school which taught cookery skills.)

Coronation chicken with rice salad

1 poached chicken or 4 large chicken breasts (you could also use a pre-cooked roast chicken)

SAUCE
¼ jar runny honey (400g jar)
3–4 spring onions
2 tbs mango chutney
1 dessertspoon curry paste
¼ cup white wine
150ml double cream, whipped
150ml thick Greek yoghurt
3–4 tbs mayonnaise

RICE SALAD
3–4 spring onions, sliced
125g mushrooms, sliced

1 cup (uncooked) rice
2–3 tomatoes, chopped
3 sticks celery, chopped
1 cucumber
½ cup frozen peas
pine nuts
2 tbsp raisins
2 tbsp herbs, parsley, chives, oregano or a mixture
3–4 tbsp vinaigrette

Mix honey, chutney, curry paste and white wine together in a small heavy pan and simmer for 10 minutes, stir well. Remove from heat and allow to cool. Stir in cream, yoghurt and mayonnaise. Cut or tear chicken into pieces and lay on a flat dish or large plate and drizzle over sauce, making sure all the chicken is covered. Decorate with toasted slivered almonds and more mango chutney.

For the rice salad, lightly fry onions and mushrooms. Mix into cooled boiled rice with chopped tomatoes, celery and cucumber. Add cooked frozen peas, toasted pine nuts and raisins. Add herbs. Dress with a vinaigrette.

SERVES 6

In that lull between Christmas and New Year's Eve we go with a group of friends to the headland at Neilsen Park, have a swim and then picnic. Everyone brings something and it's a good opportunity to finish up the ham and the Christmas cake. Eagerly anticipated are Jayne's noodle salad and Maree's onion tart.

Onion tart

PASTRY
- 125g plain flour
- 60g cold butter
- 1 egg
- salt
- iced water

FILLING
- 750g onions
- butter and oil for cooking the onions
- salt, nutmeg, pepper
- 3 egg yolks
- 150ml thick cream

Make the pastry in a food processor or by rubbing the butter into the flour, adding the egg yolk and enough water to form a dough.

Peel and slice the onions as thinly as possible. Melt butter and a little oil in a heavy frying pan. Cook the onions, covered until they are pale golden and quite soft. They must not fry and should be stirred from time to time. This will take about half an hour. Season with salt, nutmeg and pepper. Stir in the well-beaten egg yolks and the cream and leave until the time comes to cook the tart. Roll out the pastry thinly and line a 20cm oiled tart or flan tin. Pour in the filling, cook in the centre of a fairly hot oven with the tin standing on a baking sheet at 200°C for 30 minutes.

SERVES 4

Citrus noodle salad

400g–500g thin egg noodles, cooked according to the directions on the packet
olive oil

DRESSING

2 oranges, grated zest and juice
4 limes, grated zest and juice
2 tbsp brown sugar
2 tbsp rice wine vinegar
2 tbsp sesame oil
6 spring onions, finely chopped
¾ cup roasted cashew nuts or peanuts, coarsely chopped
4 tbsp olive oil
4 tbsp soy sauce
3 red chillies, deseeded and chopped
1 cup of mixed chopped herbs — basil, mint and coriander

Drizzle drained noodles with olive oil. Combine dressing ingredients, except the nuts and herbs, add these at the last minute. Dress the noodles, you can add sliced cold chicken or prawns to this salad and it is lovely served with salmon.

SERVES 6

ABBIE, WILL AND SHERRY AT MY MOTHER'S FUNERAL (2005)

Photo by Emma Hardy

Chapter Thirteen

FUNERAL BLUES

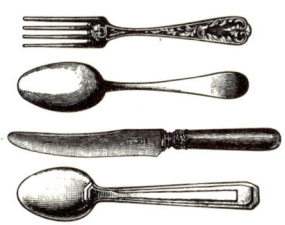

It's 2005 and I am on my way to India. On the plane to Delhi I read an Indian newspaper which reports the murder of an old woman by her son and his servant; he had bashed her, slit her throat and stuffed her body in a well. He was reported to be in a "jovial mood" answering the media's questions "boldly". We come into Delhi at night from the airport and I wonder, where are the teeming masses? The next morning Miss Joyti is our guide — a very glamorous lady in a deep fir-tree green silk shalwar kameez and matching pashmina with a lot of gold round her neck and wrists and a Dolce and Gabbana handbag. We are taken by bicycle rickshaw through the teeming narrow streets of the Old Market — monkeys everywhere climbing the electricity wires which are arranged with great ingenuity. Everything seems to be going on at once: eating, cooking, shopping, washing, sleeping. I see a men's urinal where peeing *around* it seems to be the norm, while the traffic appears to be a sort of gladiatorial battle: *Please use the horn* is painted on the back of vehicles. When we stop in traffic, little beggar girls come and paw at us. People stare, usually fairly neutrally. We visit a tomb complex built by a begum, she had a lover who was the royal jeweller so she built a tomb for him. So as to not appear too suspicious, she then had a tomb built for the royal barber as well. Her husband supposedly committed suicide, falling from a parapet of his library where he was reading, as opposed to writing, his autobiography. We also visit Ghandi's crematorium place — a huge empty park filled with the most hideous dahlias.

The next day Charlie and I leave on our tour of Rajasthan which we are doing grand luxe with a private car and a driver. Our driver is the wonderful Mr Manjit Singh, a wise and delightful man who comes highly recommended. He is not only an amazingly calm driver, but also full of ingenuity and dash when the circumstances demand; "He inspires confidence" as Mary Cook would have said. Up early in Mandawa 48 hours later and wandering out of the gate of Mandawa Castle — the huge doors are studded with spikes at elephant height (to stop the gates being charged by elephants) — we walk into the village and a shoe shop. The boy serving asks "How do you like my India?" In the fort at Bikaner, our next stop, is one of most extraordinary rooms I have ever seen; a little room painted with stylised clouds which had a sprinkler low down in one wall, the bottom half of all the walls painted with sheets of rain. Servants would have hung plants above and the Maharaja would have sat under the dripping plants and the "rain" from the sprinklers in the hot months of summer.

We eat in a restaurant called The Golden Fort, on the roof, serenaded by two musicians, one on a squeeze box and the other on drums. They sing a duet, one taking the woman's part; at the end "she" demands: "Give me, give me, give me… a lime." We have wonderful tiny beans for dinner in an unpromising looking grey sauce, but it is fragrantly delicious. In Jodhpur we have a wonderful tour of the great Fort Meherangarh. By one of the iron gates are the handprints of the wives and concubines of the Maharaja Man Singh who were *satis* in 1843. The handprints are covered in red powder and paper thin sheets of silver. Some of them are tiny.

My introduction to Indian cooking came from Ros and Madhur Jaffrey's *Indian Cookbook*. The vegetarian curry below is from Kerala where the fish and coconut curries are delicious. You can add chunks of white fish or prawns at the end or leave it as vegetarian. One of the revelations of India is how wonderful the vegetarian dishes are, with their infinite variety and delicate combinations of tastes. When you have the vegetables and lentils, and you add in the paneer and the breads and the poppadums, you really don't miss the meat. This curry looks beautiful with its yellow, red and green and it smells and tastes heavenly and fragrant with the spices. The sourness of the tamarind is perfectly balanced with the sweetness of the peas and sweet potato.

A curry always has a long list of ingredients but don't be put off, just assemble everything before you start cooking so you're not scrabbling round for the turmeric at a crucial moment.

Pea, spinach and sweet potato curry

Any self-respecting Indian housewife will grind her own spices, sometimes I do and sometimes I use ready-ground ones, the trick is to keep them sealed and replace any stale or old spices.

MARSALA SPICE MIX
    2 tsp coriander seeds or ground
    1½ tsp cumin
    1 tsp chilli powder
    ½ tsp mustard seeds
    ½ tsp white peppercorns
    ½ tsp ground turmeric

CURRY

- 2 tbs vegetable oil
- 1 large red onion, halved and thinly sliced
- 2cm fresh ginger, grated
- 2 cloves garlic, crushed
- a few curry or Kaffir lime leaves
- 2 green chillies
- 500g sweet potato, peeled and cubed
- 2 tsp brown sugar
- 4 tomatoes, quartered
- 1 tbs tamarind paste
- 400ml light coconut cream
- 150g frozen peas
- 200g spinach (I use a packet of baby spinach leaves)

Grind the spices if using whole ones, otherwise mix together. Heat the oil and add the onion, ginger, garlic and curry leaves and the whole chillies until softened but not highly coloured. Stir in the spice mix and fry until the oil separates out and the mixture smells fragrant. Stir in sweet potato, sugar, tomatoes and tamarind, followed by the coconut cream. Then refill the tin with water and add. Bring to the boil, then simmer gently until the sweet potato is cooked, about 25–30 minutes. Stir in the peas and cook for 5 minutes. Add the spinach and cook until it wilts.

Serve with steamed rice.

SERVES 4

Indian shepherd's pie

- 3 large Spanish onions, sliced thinly
- 3 cups cooked roast lamb, chopped
- 2 ripe tomatoes

2 tbs vinegar
1 cup coriander leaves
1 cup mint leaves

If you have the foresight, save any gravy leftover from the lamb roast.

MARSALA

1 tbs ground coriander
1 tsp ground cumin
2 cloves garlic
2 dried chillies
½ teaspoon mustard seed
2cm fresh ginger, chopped or grated
4 small shallots, sliced

Fry sliced onion until brown in a frying pan in vegetable oil, remove and fry marsala ingredients until aromatic. Put fried onions back in the pan, add the tomatoes diced and the meat and any leftover gravy and the vinegar and add salt to taste. Make sure everything is very hot and the tomatoes have softened a little, remove from heat and stir in herbs.

Serve with rice or better still dahl.

SERVES 4

Dahl curry

225g red splint lentils, washed
2 garlic cloves, crushed
2.5cm fresh ginger, grated
2–3 green chillies, deseeded and finely chopped
½ teaspoon ground turmeric
½ teaspoon ground cumin
1 tsp ground coriander

250ml coconut milk
1 tomato, roughly chopped
1 tbs oil
½ tsp mustard seeds
1 tsp cumin seeds
1 onion, finely chopped
10 curry seeds
quantity spinach leaves
2 tbsp fresh coriander

Put lentils in a pan with 500ml water and bring to the boil. Now add garlic, ginger, turmeric, cumin, coriander, coconut milk and tomato. Bring all this to the boil and simmer 10 minutes.

Heat oil in a frying pan. Add mustard and cumin seeds and fry until seeds are popping. Add onion and curry seeds and cook until onion is soft and golden, about 10 minutes. Stir this mixture into the lentils. Cook another 10 minutes or so and lastly stir in washed spinach leaves and coriander.

Serves 4

On the way to Udaipur we stop at a Jain temple in Rankapur and are given a slightly cursory tour by the high priest who glows with health and sanctity — his saffron robes slightly undermined by rather dreary blue-grey socks. The temple complex is 400 years old but was devastated by the Mughals and abandoned, the only worshippers — including his ancestors, according to the priest — coming by bullock cart and horse to worship at the full moon. A British officer, exploring at the time of the Raj, found the Temple, overgrown with creepers and falling down. Now it is restored with hundreds of complexly carved pillars. No two pillars are the same and one is on a distinct lean to show only God is perfect, man always has imperfections. The two Jain tenets are "live and let live" and "forgive and forget". On the way out of the temple, meticulously swept every morning lest a spider or an ant should be inadvertently squashed (Jains protect all forms of life) a woman gives me a rose and a sprig of mint.

The Lake Palace at Udaipur is beautiful and luxurious. In our beautiful carved, brocade-covered bed we watch "The Golden Globes" on TV. We are also amused by the comments of the American tourists around us: : "I lost my Imodium" and "It's a nice room but it isn't a suite."

We move onto Pushkar, the holy city — so holy no meat, eggs or alcohol are allowed in the city. There are lots of hippies wandering round staying in ashrams. I suppose I am fascinated by religious observance because I'm not religious — faith made manifest is very interesting, especially when it is as incomprehensibly complex as in India. Who are all these incarnations and why would the same deity have so many names and forms? Christianity seems a doddle to get your head around, by comparison. At one temple I see worshippers pass their hands over a flame, then pass that hand over their face and forehead, washing in the flame. I see a tiny boy copying his mother and doing this.

And it's here in Pushkar at breakfast, in the gloom of the hotel dining room, that a phone rings and it's my daughter Daisy with the news that my mother is dead.

Saul Bellow, that wise old bird, compared losing a parent to driving through a plate glass window. In a letter to Martin Amis, after Kingsley's death, he wrote "…you didn't know it was there until it shattered and then for years to come you're picking up the pieces, down to the last glassy splinter." (Letter to Martin Amis, March 13th 1996).

Robert's death, in June 1992, came more or less out of the blue. I found out long afterwards he had said his goodbyes about a week before to the receptionist in the doctor's surgery. There was some mention of an investigative medical procedure, and perhaps wishing to avoid that or worrying about it, brought on the stroke that killed him. In photos taken on his birthday, about a week before he died, the light has gone out of his eyes — those twinkling blue eyes, always so alight with mischief. My brother Sheridan rang to say Robert had had a stroke and then rang again on a winter Sydney dawn to say "We've lost him."

Of all the euphemisms I find "we've lost him/her" to be the most irritating. We hadn't lost him, implying he could be found again, he was dead.

We went to England, as planned, about six weeks after Robert died, to a house where his absence was palpable. There were no mementos but I took one of his hats. In the Colt House, the little writing hut down by the swimming pool, the smell of his cigars still hung in the air.

Now, it is 15 years later and my mother has died, at home in her bed with an ambulance on its way.

In Pushkar, Mr Manjit asks me what I want to do, offering to drive straight back to Delhi. We decide to go on to the next stop in our itinerary; we are staying in some huge colonial pile now a hotel and one of the Taj chain. We are greeted by a young woman in a sari who takes our passports, organises all the checking in and the luggage and shows us to our palatial room. On the way she enquires what the matter is with my eyes. "Oh," I say, "I've just heard that my mother is dead and I've been weeping."

"How old are you, madam?" she asks brightly, "50, 60, 70?" I indicate that 60 is about right.

She replies: "I think you are very lucky, you had your mother for a very long time. I am orphan child." Well, as they say, there is really no answer to that and she is absolutely right.

A few days earlier we had been on the flat roof of a building that was being used as a school. The children had recited, apparently in English but so rapidly it was almost unintelligible, what I think was the fable of the ant and grasshopper or possibly the fox and the grapes. While this was going on there was a commotion down below and we went to the edge of the roof to look down into the unpaved street. A group were running along, chanting, and there was the sound of drums and cymbals. It was a funeral our guide told us and sure enough, there was a body being carried aloft, wrapped but with the face exposed — a little brown wizened face under a knitted beanie, with coins on the eyes. I said something to the effect that it sounded quite joyous — not solemn and sad. "This is an old one," said our guide, "we do not grieve for old ones, only for the young — a life unfulfilled."

Afterwards, of course, one looks for signs, for premonitions; I had said goodbye to Joan so many times, always thinking through my tears as we drove to the airport, that's it, I'll never see her again. And so many times I walked through the back door to find her in her dressing gown waiting for me on an English summer morning.

When I breezed in on my annual visits from Australia and tried to instigate a new fridge or replace tattered curtains or a sagging mattress she fought against any change, however small.

A couple of years before she died my mother had a fall. My aunt Sally nobly held the fort until I could get over from Sydney.

I had always said to my brothers that I would be the one who would "deal with things" when the moment came.

I discovered she had lost her, up to then, firm grip on the finances. Her solicitor had retired without passing her on to anyone else and her "financial advisor" seemed negligent to an almost criminal degree. I found four bank accounts (all overdrawn to the max), a dwindling cache of shares, and various annuities including a mysterious but extremely welcome US pension still being paid to her from Robert's US earnings. Naturally, there was nothing like a friendly, or even an unfriendly, bank manager to ask for advice. That she had had a bank account with Lloyds since her 21st birthday meant nothing to whoever I finally got to speak to. The local branch of Barclays was slightly more approachable but unable to extend any credit.

I did some sums and flew a kite without much hope of its lifting off the ground. The house was very expensive to run. Six bedrooms, three bathrooms, a kitchen, and four ground floor rooms, albeit small ones, meant the ancient boiler consumed the heating oil at a terrifying rate. Would she consider moving, perhaps to Henley-on-Thames, a little house, walking distance to the shops, cosy, all new appliances, no acreage to worry about keeping up, no swimming pool to worry about? She looked at me as if I had lost my mind, "Oh, I don't think I'd want to move, darling," she said. "You see this house is so easy to run and so economical." I pretended I had left something on the stove and escaped to the kitchen where I shut the door. Should I scream, laugh hysterically or have a gin and tonic?

An old friend, the director Frith Banbury, came to the rescue. A firm called Northern Rock offered something called a reverse mortgage. My brother Will came over from his home in Tampa, Florida and, with my mother's permission, we re-arranged Joan's life.

Sally discovered a godsend, an agency who would send young women for a couple of months at a time (usually Australians or New Zealanders or South Africans) who would be prepared to live in the depths of Berkshire in an old-fashioned house and cook and shop and be company for a woman in her 90s. So, after that fall, we set up a support system and, rather surprisingly, it all worked pretty smoothly. For three years a succession of youngish women came to live at "Fairmans" for three to six months and shopped, drove and cooked. It was mostly a huge success. The agency was very good at finding young women for whom the isolation of being in the English countryside was a plus rather than a minus. When I visited I immediately gave them time off but within 24 hours I would be wondering how on earth I could stand another day.

And then she died. "Stay a few more days," said my brother Will, over from Florida, and coping with it all. "We can have the funeral next week. Stay and see the Taj Mahal. Ma would want you to."

But now I'm back at "Fairmans" and we are on our way to the crematorium; it's half past nine on a cold January morning. In the back of the car are me, my brother Wilton and my sister in law, Ruth. Her husband, my brother Sheridan, is in the front passenger seat. The car is being driven by John Jonas, who was originally my father's chauffeur and his dresser in the theatre. When Robert stopped acting John took a job with a local businessman but since his own retirement and my father's death, he has kept an eye on the house and the garden and, most importantly, on my mother. John knows all the family secrets, and I assume a few things about my father's life probably no one else knows. Most importantly today he is the person who knows how to get us to the crematorium — through the nightmare one way systems the civic planners have imposed on the quiet Berkshire towns of my childhood.

The night before the funeral the vicar talked us through the day's rituals. He has had a revolutionary idea, instead of the hiatus imposed by the family having to accompany the coffin to the crematorium after the funeral service, leaving the mourners to cool their heels, as it were, we are cremating my mother first then having the service around the ashes in the afternoon, followed by the funeral tea.

We find the crematorium, my brothers having been mostly silent while Ruth has kept up a chatty stream of conversation and I have sat transfixed (as usual) by what she is wearing: Persian lamb. Her late mother's coat, I am informed. Ruth's taste in clothes tends towards the theatrical. She got my brother out of the rather nondescript clothes he favoured and into silk shirts, suede jackets and even an identity bracelet and a signet ring.

There is a list pinned up. My mother's name is at the top of the list, only it's not quite correct. My mother's name is JOAN NORTH MORLEY and this says JOAN NORAH MORLEY. I foresee endless complications; what about the order of service for the funeral, will the name be wrong on that as well? I confront a smallish man, who looks official. "This is wrong," I say, "You've got her name wrong, it isn't Norah, it's North, she would have hated to be Norah." In rather aggrieved tones he tells me that the name is taken from the Death Certificate so it's impossible that it's incorrect. I tell him my brother and I attended to the death certificate and that obviously we got that *right*. My voice is rising somewhat and I can see my brothers backing away. The official looking man says, plaintively: "Madam, I'm only a bearer." Luckily at this moment the vicar arrives so I tell him about the mix up. He roars with laughter. "On the order of service, the printer put JOHN NORTH MORLEY," he says merrily. "Mind you, he is a bit dyslexic."

Meanwhile the hearse has turned up and the undertaker is waiting to show me the flowers. I had specified white lilies and greenery and on no account any baby's breath. Had it been summer we would have had lilies of the valley, her favourite flower.

The brief service is strangely surreal. Is my mother really lying in that coffin, dressed in the clothes I picked out?

In minutes we are back in the car and I ask Will if he has organised the champagne for the funeral tea, knowing full well he hasn't. So we stop at the local supermarket. I suggest that not everyone needs to get out of the car, but before the words are out of my mouth we are all heading for the entrance. Sheridan, slightly out of it, suffering as he does from severe depression and rattling with the pills he takes to alleviate it, mutters something about needing light bulbs. Ruth has decided she is making everyone scrambled eggs and smoked salmon for lunch, so she heads off to buy those. Will heads for the wine section. When he gets there, I hear a shriek of "Eleven quid, and it isn't even vintage." Being a restaurateur, he is used to wholesale prices. Eventually we all head back to the car.

At the funeral, Sherry is to kick off the proceedings with the eulogy. I have seen him wandering about the house in the interim between the cremation and the church service, muttering, with several pieces of paper in his hand. It occurs to me that I should check with him what he is going to say. But he is so hen-pecked by Ruth that I think, "Oh hell, leave it, let him say what he likes." One of my nieces is reading the passage from Ecclesiastes 3:4 about there being a time for everything: "a time to weep and a time to mourn". I am reading "Fear no more the heat of the sun" from *Cymbeline*.

Sherry's opening observation is that my mother was the god daughter of J.M. Barrie, creator of *Peter Pan*. As Sherry announces this, there is a sharp intake of breath from Sally, behind me, and her daughter Justine says quite loudly "No, Mummy *you* were!" My brother Will turns to me, "*Was* she?" "No," I whisper, "Sal was." (My aunt Sally was born 20 years or so later after my mother, after G had played *Peter Pan* and become friends with Barrie.)

Sherry's whole eulogy is posited on the fact that Joannie, like *Peter Pan*, never grew old. I think "well, does it really matter, it's only the people in this church that are hearing it." Then of course, never wasteful, Sherry arranges to have it printed in the *Spectator*. I never asked him if he really thought she was Barrie's godchild or if he just changed the facts to make a good story, or was just confused.

My cousin Emma takes a picture of the house as the guests arrive for the funeral tea. Joan's old friend Mary Cook, frail on her two sticks, is being greeted at the front door by me, the windows are lit and the light shines out into the dark garden, only my mother's bedroom is dark.

I am pleased with my choice of Ivor Novello singing "We'll Gather Lilacs" as we file out of the church. Ivor and my grandmother were great friends, Ivor stayed at "Charlwood" the house my mother lived in as a child with G. But I am still brooding on the eulogy.

When everyone has gone I say to Will "Next time, I don't think we'll let Sherry read something we haven't proofed." And he replies, gently, "Darling, there isn't going to be a next time."

After the funeral the estate agents send three young people, two women and a man to look at the house and the grounds, eleven acres, nine of them woods. One of the women joins me in the kitchen; the central heating was playing up and the house is freezing. The kitchen with the Aga merrily burning through the incredibly expensive oil is just about bearable.

"Super house," says the young woman brightly, peering through the windows out onto the desolate January garden. "Super views, may I ask why it's going on the market?"

"Neither of my brothers nor I want to live here." I say. This is not strictly true, we are all in our different ways going to feel a chill with the loss of "Fairmans".

A shadow crosses her face "It's not, gosh…" she hesitates, "it's not a deceased estate is it?"

"Yes, it is," I say rather sharply, "My mother."

"Gosh, I'm sorry.." she pauses again. "When did she die?"

"Do you know," I say, "I haven't the faintest idea." And the funny thing is, at that moment I *hadn't* the faintest idea, a week, ten days, two weeks, I couldn't have told you. Something had happened to my brain.

But then there are the memories, many of them of food.

For my mother's birthday one July summer's day, Sherry and Ruth gave a lunch party in their house in Chelsea Harbour. I made the birthday cake, chocolate roulade, filled with raspberries. A roulade is like a Swiss roll and I made two, put them on a pretty dish and decorated them with tiny pink roses. I left the cakes in Ruth's kitchen and when I went to get them, a large slice had been cut from the end of one. Ruth's helper in the kitchen told me the culprit was "Mr Sammy", Ruth's father, who had taken a slice with him and gone to watch the cricket on TV somewhere in the house. Luckily for Mr Sammy I was able to even the cakes up and cover the gap with a few more roses. As for many, many sweet things I have found a dusting of icing sugar covers a multitude of sins.

Chocolate roulade

5 eggs, separated
180g castor sugar
180g dark chocolate
icing sugar
cream to fill
raspberries, fresh or frozen

Beat egg yolks and sugar until thick and pale. Melt chocolate, cool slightly and add to egg yolks and sugar. Beat egg whites until stiff and fold into chocolate mixture. Spread in a Swiss roll tin lined with kitchen paper. Bake 15 minutes at 180°C or until cake looks set. Take out of the oven and cover immediately with a clean wet tea towel. Leave until cool, then turn out on baking paper dusted with icing sugar. Spread with whipped cream, add raspberries if desired and, using the paper to help you, roll up. Put on a plate, seam side down and dust with more icing sugar. The cake is very delicate and may well crack but it should hold together. Refrigerate until serving.

SERVES 6

Charlie

Wedding day (18th September 1976)

Chapter Fourteen

MY FATHER'S HOUSE

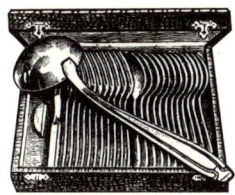

At my mother's funeral Sherry said: "We can't go home anymore." Although we each had perfectly good homes, Sherry in London, Will in Tampa, Florida and me in Sydney, we all knew what he meant. I have now lived in one flat and two houses which have been my own. In London and in Sydney I have drawn curtains when night fell, sat with friends and children round a table for Sunday lunch, drunk tea in the garden, sometimes even on a lawn, under a tree.

What my children, and Sherry's children and grandchildren particularly liked about "Fairmans" was the constancy. My mother kept old toys and books in what had been our playroom and then became my sitting room, the books showed signs of wear and tear but there they were. The plastic doll's tea set to be taken out and played with, splashing water from the teapot onto the carpet. They read the copy of *Milly Molly Mandy* whose illustrations had been crudely coloured in and on whose flyleaf was printed in large letters, running down the page: ANNABEL MORLEY.

I don't keep things to the same extent that Joannie did but there are a lot of photos, capturing moments in time. There are also the books my mother kept for us plus the actual published ones written by G, Buck, Robert and Sherry. And, of course, there are the DVDs. A neighbour once casually remarked that he had seen an old film with Robert in it on TV recently and I said I had, too. "Is it creepy, seeing and hearing your father?" he asked. The answer is no, it isn't creepy; it's nostalgic and rather astonishing when I realise that in most of those films he's younger than I am now.

Robert chose films very often because they were going to be made in a part of the world he thought he'd like to see: Austria, Spain, Turkey, India or Russia. When I went later to Turkey I remembered him telling us about a picnic on the Bosphorus with a champion lady sculler and delicious bread and honey. Robert loved chatting to everyone when he was abroad. He liked to pick the locals' brains: where should he go, what should he see, who ran the best restaurant? If he was recognised, all to the good. Only on the race course when he was concentrating on the form did he sometimes slightly baulk at being engaged in conversation. When other film stars sometimes mourned their loss of anonymity, Robert would say "The time to start fussing is when they *don't* recognise you."

He made the film *The Blue Bird* with Elizabeth Taylor in Russia. One night, stuck in a rather gloomy hotel she bemoaned the fact that she couldn't go out without being mobbed by fans. "Nonsense, darling," said Robert, "put on a headscarf and we'll go out and have a lovely dinner somewhere. No one will recognise you." She put the diamond as big as the Ritz on her finger and they sallied forth. As they were being shown to their table in the restaurant, the normally phlegmatic Muscovites were craning their necks, laying aside their table napkins, standing up and in the further corners of the room beginning to climb on the tables to get a better view of Miss Taylor. Hustled back to the hotel by security Elizabeth remarked wistfully,

"I did tell you I couldn't go out without being recognised," took off the diamond, replaced it in the hotel safe in reception and went hungry to her suite.

Summer wedding

England in 1976 had a phenomenally long hot summer; there were water restrictions, deep cracks appeared in our parched gardens, the sun shone day after day. I selfishly wanted the weather to hold as Charlie and I were getting married in a marquee in mid-September on what had once been the croquet lawn. Since Charlie was in Australia, the planning fell to me. I sent him a telegram: *Have booked the vicar and the caterers, may I book you for September 18th?*

Robert was pleased with the sensible advice of the wine merchant who was supplying the champagne, serve a decent one to start with and then go on to something less expensive. "May I suggest that, if the occasion is to be al fresco," said the vintner, "your guests will be none the wiser."

However, he was slightly miffed that he had a non-speaking part in the ceremony; mostly because he had to leave for his Saturday matinee of *How The Other Half Loves* before the cutting of the cake and the speeches.

Charlie and I spent our wedding night at a hotel in Sonning, on the River Thames called "The French Horn". It was like a set for a Feydeau farce, all red velvet and gilt. In the morning we drove back to "Fairmans" to pick up our wedding presents and say goodbye to my parents before we went back to London and then off on honeymoon to France and Italy. Having loaded up the car we were about to say goodbye when my Great Aunt Gracie, who was deaf, came hurrying over. She clearly wanted to tell my mother something of great import, tugging at her sleeve and saying "Man, man in tent."

So we all trooped off towards the almost empty marquee. Empty that is except for a tramp who was lying under one of caterer's trestle tables, wrapped in his old coat, sound asleep.

My mother gave him a slight nudge with her foot, "Can we help you?" she said. "A cup of tea would be nice," replied the tramp who had apparently spent the summer moving from venue to venue following the tent suppliers as they raised marquees for summer weddings, flower shows and country house garden parties.

Tuscan idyll

The honeymoon was our first taste of Italy together, Chianti in fact, not Tuscany where we have spent so many subsequent summers. A great part of the pleasure of Italy is cooking and eating. Elizabeth Romer's wonderfully evocative book *The Tuscan Year* draws on the memories, traditions and recipes of a woman, Silvana Cerotti who farms with her family in "a green and secret valley" on the border of Tuscany and Umbria. I regularly cook roast chicken in the Tuscan manner from this book, which simply means chopping sage leaves and crushing garlic, mixing this with salt and cubed cold butter which is inserted carefully between the skin and the flesh of the chicken's breast and pushed into the joint where the legs meet the body. With her recipe "Chicken with sage and garlic" I serve what I think of as Tuscan potatoes. Cube and parboil potatoes or use small "chats", then toss in olive oil and crushed garlic, add rosemary branches and cook as for roast potatoes, in a hot oven. Roasted Roma tomatoes are also good with this.

If you happen to be in Tuscany in autumn, you will hear a lot of shooting going on and see groups of men, immaculately attired in varieties of camouflage with smart little Alpine type hats with feathers in the hat band, walking with dogs and shotguns and basically shooting at anything. Small songbirds, thrushes and blackbirds are part of this annual slaughter, as are rabbits and hares — nothing is safe from the hunters, right up to the alarming looking wild boar which are made into endless varieties of salami . If you see "cinghiale" on a menu, perhaps in a pasta sauce, order it. Boar meat, so Elizabeth Romer states, has a more subtle flavour than ordinary pork.

In September 2001, Charlie and I stayed for three months in the Crete Senesi, that almost lunar landscape, near Siena. My cousins, the Brownes, had bought a house there in the 1970s, a house called La Fornace. Fornace is a house I dream about, a farm house lovingly and beautifully restored by another cousin, Gordon Neale. After the summer guests have gone, the house is closed up and so Charlie and I lived in the *Fienile*, a little square box of a house, like a child's drawing, which had originally been the hay store. It consisted of a bedroom upstairs, a room downstairs which was living room and kitchen, a separate bathroom and for heat, a wood burning stove. No telephone, no television but sometimes an English Sunday paper and occasionally a very crackly bit of the BBC World Service. We could sit outside and eat lunch at an old marble table right into November.

Autumnal Tuscany is wind in the cypresses and the grey, green olive trees standing heavy with their fruit, looking blasted and gnarled. Serried rows of vines with dusty bunches of grapes are in the vineyards until the *vendemmia*. In the fields the earth is turned into huge, dusty clods of the pale, clay-heavy soil which will hang together until the earth freezes, then break into little pieces, holding the moisture. A few sheep can be glimpsed, huddled in the shadow of a hill. The hills are every shade of brown, golden, grey-brown, ochre and taupe and the cypresses look black against them in the afternoon light. In the afternoon the wind often drops and stillness comes. In the garden the greenest thing is the rosemary, the lavender is dried and cut, only hips remain on the rose bushes. But the fig trees around the swimming pool are still magnificently bearing fruit.

In October we picked the olives from the neglected olive trees in the garden and booked a slot to have them crushed at the Frantoio, the olive press, which operates around the clock at the time of the olive harvest. The oil was wonderful, thick, green and a little spicy. We even managed to bring a little bottle back to Sydney, though getting it through customs in Los Angeles took some determination and diplomacy.

One day at the baker's in Montisi, the village that is closest to Fornace, we saw a sign advertising a Rabbit Feast, to raise funds for one of the local contradas. Like Siena, Montisi has rival contradas, I suppose the word parish or neighbourhood approximates to it. You are born into a contrada and that is then where your allegiance lies.

We joined an assortment of the locals on the appointed night, the man who owned one of the local restaurants, couples with small bored children, a few babies and grannies and some smarter people from Siena, the women all serpentine hair and jewellery with bosom displaying tops. There was much jollity and the courses kept coming. We ate crostini, little squares of toasted bread with an indefinable topping which tasted vaguely fishy but must have been bunny, served with olives and surrounded by pieces of fried minced rabbit. Then we ate pappadelle with a rabbit ragu, a risotto with rabbit livers, rabbit with artichokes, lemony and delicious. Then out came a rolled nut of rabbit with a rich sauce, then rabbit *agro dolce* which included currants and was served with mashed potato. Then rabbit cacciatore with polenta, fried rabbit with a much needed salad and finally a rabbit-shaped ice cream cake. We drank with all of this two delicious wines: a Friuli Sauvignon and a young Brunello. I still love rabbit, although it took a few months to be able to face eating it after the feast.

In the splendid COOP supermarket in Sinalunga you can buy

pieces of rabbit, at a pinch you can cook a whole one like this, but pieces are easier. This is how Patricia Leehy, a wonderful friend and a wonderful cook, cooks rabbit.

Rabbit with mustard and cream

2 medium sized onions or 4–6 shallots
3 rashers bacon, chopped into pieces
1–2 tbsp olive oil
50g butter
1 rabbit, jointed
2–3 tbsp Dijon mustard
flour to dust rabbit joints
2–3 tbsp white wine
2–3 tbsp chicken stock
3–4 tbsp cream

Fry onions or shallots and bacon (in Italy I use pancetta, which comes already diced) in a mixture of olive oil and butter. Then add the rabbit or rabbit pieces which you have first patted dry on kitchen paper, then smeared with smooth Dijon mustard and then floured. Make sure the rabbit is browned all over then add white wine and chicken stock. Season well with salt and pepper and cook until the rabbit is tender. You can do this in an oven or on top of the stove. It needs to cook gently for perhaps an hour. Take out the rabbit and as much of the bacon and onion as you can. Add some more mustard, say a tablespoon, to the cooking juices and stir in cream.

This is very good when served with mashed potato and green beans or a green salad.

SERVES 4

Tomatoes and peaches are the best they can be in Tuscany. The incredibly simple tomato bruschetta can start every meal as far as I'm concerned, I never tire of it. I don't even add basil but you could. Tuscans often just serve slices of bread, grilled which have been rubbed with olive oil and garlic. Of course, you need good bread and good oil, but cover the grilled bread with chopped tomatoes, a good slosh of olive oil, salt, pepper and a pinch of sugar and you have tomato bruschetta. You can add chopped basil and garlic.

Antipasto is another wonderful way to start a meal.

Antipasto

Melon and prosciutto — standards of prosciutto vary enormously, taste a sliver before you buy, it can be very dry and chewy.

White beans and tuna — (the best canned tuna is Sirena in olive oil) and a can of cannellini beans, drained and rinsed. Make a vinaigrette with lots of mustard, olive oil and lemon. Finely chop red onion and mix together.

Bocconcini or buffalo mozzarella, sliced avocado and tomatoes.

Grilled aubergine (eggplant).

Asparagus — cooked and then dressed with vinaigrette while warm.

Salami and an Italian cheese, Pecorino is good.

A handful of olives.

Bread sticks.

There are a few vegetables to cook, a bit of chopping and mixing but this looks wonderful, each thing on a small platter or put together on a large one.

This can be a lunch in itself or a substantial first course, follow it with something not too heavy like fish or chicken.

Below is an unusual first course, which owes a passing nod to those mustard fruits you can buy in beautiful blue and white jars in Italy. It is a sort of fruit salad but it's easy and a good way to start a meal in which the second course will be something richly substantial.

Fruit with prosciutto and red wine-mustard sauce

150ml red wine
60g castor sugar
1 bay leaf
1–2 tbsp of smooth Dijon mustard
¼ ripe melon, sliced
1–2 pears, skin on or off as you prefer, sliced
2 figs, sliced
2 plums, sliced
some black grapes, pips removed

Simmer wine, sugar and bay leaf over a moderate heat for 5 mins cool and then mix in mustard. Pour this over the sliced fruit. Serve with prosciutto.

SERVES 4

I don't think Italians are very good at puddings with the exception of gelato. Tiramisu can be delicious but it can also be a sticky, sickly disappointment. The coffee needs to be strong and the amount of sugar small. This is the recipe my daughter Daisy uses.

Tiramisu

250ml cream
4 eggs, separated
½ cup castor sugar
250g mascarpone
⅓ cup Kahlua (coffee liqueur)
28 sponge finger biscuits (Savoiardi)
500ml freshly brewed coffee, cooled
1 tbs sieved cocoa to dust on top

Combine egg yolks and sugar in a bowl, whisk until thick and pale, then fold in mascarpone. Whisk cream and fold in. Whisk egg whites, until you have soft peaks and fold into mascarpone/egg yolk mixture. Add Kahlua to coffee, dip biscuits in Kahlua/coffee mixture, and place in a layer on the bottom of a deep serving dish. Spread mascarpone mixture over and repeat process until all ingredients have been used up, ending with a mascarpone layer. Refrigerate at least 4 hours or overnight. Dust with cocoa before serving.

SERVES 8

A wonderful, easy dessert is affogato. This is just a scoop or two of the best vanilla ice cream you can buy with a tiny expresso coffee poured over and a shot of Frangelico (or any other liqueur you like).

A particularly Tuscan finish to a meal is biscotti (little hard biscuits) and Vin Santo. Vin Santo (Holy Wine) is a fortified sweet wine, in fact it can be quite dry like a good sherry. The little hard almond biscuits are dipped into it. The following recipe makes a lot of little biscuits but they keep almost indefinitely.

Biscotti di prato

3 cups plain flour
1 tsp baking powder
1½ cups castor sugar
a pinch of salt
2 eggs, beaten
250g shelled almonds, chopped

Sift flour and baking powder together. Combine all ingredients; you may need a bit more egg. The mixture should just hold together, form into 2 long loaves about 2.5cm high and 10cm wide. Brush tops with beaten egg and bake in a slow oven (160°C) for about 20 minutes. When cool enough cut diagonally into thin slices and bake these again (180°C) for 20 minutes or so. Serve with little glasses of a dessert wine and/or coffee.

MAKES ABOUT 40

England

In 2008 Tesco, a British supermarket chain, surveyed 100 adults and found that certain traditional British dishes such as steak and kidney pudding and jam roly-poly are rarely made from scratch and people are far more likely to cook curries or pasta dishes. Spotted dick, beef Wellington, Coronation chicken, sherry trifle and Lancashire hotpot: "are prepared so infrequently that they could disappear from the national menu in little more than a decade." (*The Weekly Telegraph*, 12–18 March 2008).

The *Telegraph* also reported that schools have had to take the place of "the institutions that used to set the boundaries of acceptable behaviour — fundamentally church and family. One of the most important factors has been the loss of the family meal which has reduced family conversation."

One thing Robert always insisted on was people making conversation when we all sat round the table for Sunday lunch, whether it was at home or out. When, later in life, he had a hearing aid, he would leave it turned off unless he thought the conversation was sufficiently interesting. The great director Tyrone Guthrie's mantra was "Astonish me", Robert's was "Amuse me".

I have been pondering why "Fairmans" had such a hold over me, a house is only bricks and tiles, lathe and plaster and in the case of "Fairmans", wood and terracotta. One of the prospective estate agents said to us: "Of course, whoever buys it will want to knock it down and rebuild ."He didn't get the gig. But it's not our house anymore. Why did I, do I care?

Bruce Springsteen sings about a dream of going back to his father's house. When he wakes up the next day he drives to the house and a strange woman opens the door; in answer to his query she tells him no one by that name lives here anymore.

I drove past "Fairmans" two years ago, the orchard was still there the house was still there but the shutters had gone, the front door had been moved and there was a new rather smart gate. In what had been the nursery, there was a vase of flowers on the window sill. Do the people who live there now sometimes have tea on the lawn and then move everything inside before the cushions and the chairs get damp as evening falls? Does a father offer everyone a drink and a mother tell the children what time supper will be and ask them to tidy up the Sunday papers? If guests are departing do they somewhat reluctantly leave but with a bunch of roses and sweetpeas and a lettuce or two, driving off through the soft summer twilight as the curtains are drawn and the house settles itself around the people who live there? I hope so.

SUMMER 1956

RECIPE INDEX

Antipasto 244
Apple
  herring, apple and beetroot salad 159
  horseradish sauce 25
  sausage, apple and cranberry stuffing 196
Beans
  cassoulet 175
Béchamel sauce 22, 75
Beef
  bollito misto 172
Beetroot
  herring, apple and beetroot salad 159
  roast 158
Biscuits
  biscotti di prato 247
  spiced Christmas stars 210
Boiled fruit cake 205
Bollito misto 172
Bread
  bread and butter pudding, marmalade 32
  Chekhovian cucumber sandwiches 84
  chicken sandwiches 135
  wholemeal banana bread 83
Buttermilk vichyssoise 213
Cakes
  boiled fruit cake 205
  certosino 204
  chocolate brownies 66
  chocolate roulade 235
  farmhouse teabread 82
  glacé Christmas 203
  orange 84
  Sachertorte 118

truffle terrine 67
wholemeal banana bread 83
Caramel sauce 16
Cassoulet 175
Certosino 204
Cheese
  caramelised onion and goats' cheese tartlets 208
  soufflé, twice baked 178
Chekhovian cucumber sandwiches 84
Cherry sauce 120
Chicken
  coronation chicken with rice salad 216
  en cocotte 144
  fricassee 75
  liver pâté 72
  pork and veal terrine with cherry sauce 120
  roast with pumpkin and black lentils 42
  sandwiches 135
  terrine 73
  two-minute roast chicken stuffing 41
Chocolate
  brownies 66
  French truffles 209
  pecan pie 124
  petit pots du chocolat 68
  roulade 235
  truffle terrine 67
Christmas cooking
  cake, glacé 203
  pudding 200, 201
  spiced stars 210
Citrus noodle salad 219
Colcannon 98
Cold parsleyed ham 199
Coronation chicken with rice salad 216
Crème brûlée 20
Crème caramel 21
Cucumber
  green pea 213
  Lebanese soup 212

sandwiches 84
Curry
  dahl 225
  kedgeree 143
  pea, spinach and sweet potato 223
  prawn and tomato 109
  Thakkali 109
Dahl curry 225
Desserts *see also* Puddings
  crème brûlée 20
  crème caramel 21
  crunchy lime semifreddo 162
  honey and raspberry panna cotta 164
  lemon posset 19
  panna cotta 163
  petit pots du chocolat 68
  raspberry hazelnut meringue 91
  semifreddo al torrone (nougat semifreddo) 161
  tiramisu 246
Duck with oranges or cherries 99
Farmhouse teabread 82
Fish
  herring, apple and beetroot salad 159
  pie 22
  Scandinavian baked ocean trout with apple and horseradish sauce 25
  smoked salmon pancakes 207
  stuffed sardines 24
French truffles 209
Fricadelles (meatballs), veal and pork 136
Fricassee, chicken 75
Fruit with prosciutto and red wine-mustard sauce 245
Gazpacho 122
Glacé Christmas cake 203
Gnocchi, semolina 160
Golden syrup and lime tart 15
Green pea soup 213

Ham, cold parsleyed 199
Herring, apple and beetroot salad 159
Honey and raspberry panna cotta 164
Icing, orange 85
Indian shepherd's pie 224
Kedgeree 143
Lamb
    Easter lamb with garlic and herbs 58
    spring roast with mint yoghurt sauce 52
Lebanese cucumber soup 212
Lemons
    posset 19
    tarte au citron 189
Lime
    citrus noodle salad 219
    crunchy semifreddo 162
    golden syrup tart 15
Lombardy turkey 197
Marmalade
    bread and butter pudding 32
    David Mabey's dark coarse cut marmalade 53
Marsala 225
Meringue, raspberry hazelnut 91
Mint yoghurt sauce 52
Nougat semifreddo 161
Onion
    goats' cheese tartlets 208
    tart 218
Orange
    Boodle's fool 18
    cake 84
    citrus noodle salad 219
    David Mabey's dark coarse cut marmalade 53
    duck with oranges or cherries 99
    marmalade bread and butter pudding 32
Oven risotto 174
Pancakes, smoked salmon 207
Panna cotta 163
    honey and raspberry 164
Panzanella 33
Pasta
    semolina gnocchi 160
Pâté, chicken liver 72
Pea, spinach and sweet potato curry 223
Peaches, spiced 209
Pecan and chocolate pie 124
Petit pots du chocolat 68
Picada 43
Pies and pastries (savoury)
    caramelised onion and goats' cheese tartlets 208
    fish pie 22
    onion tart 218
    tomato pissaladiere 215
Pies and pastries (sweet)
    chocolate and pecan pie 124
    lime and golden syrup tart 15
    pate sable (short crust) 189
    tarte au citron 189
Pissaladiere 215
Plums
    queen of plums pudding 14
    roasted 163
Pork
    chicken and veal terrine with cherry sauce 120
    veal fricadelles (meatballs) 136
Potatoes
    buttermilk vichyssoise 213
    colcannon 98
    salad 198
    salmorejo 214
Prawns
    potted 126
    tomato curry 109
Puddings
    Christmas 200, 201
    marmalade bread and butter 32
    orange Boodle's fool 18
    queen of plums 14
    sticky date 16
Pumpkin and black lentils, roast chicken with 42
Queen of plums pudding 14
Rabbit with mustard and cream 243
Raspberry
    hazelnut meringue 91
    honey panna cotta 164
Rice salad 216
Risotto, oven 174
Roasted plums 163
Roulade, chocolate 235
Sachertorte 118
Salads
    citrus noodle 219
    fruit with prosciutto and red wine-mustard sauce 245
    herring, apple and beetroot salad 159
    Panzanella 33
    potato 198
    rice 216
    Thai beef 139
Salmorejo 214
Salsa verde 173
Sandwiches, chicken 135
Sardines, stuffed 24
Sauces and dressings
    apple and horseradish sauce 25
    béchamel sauce 22, 75
    caramel sauce 16
    cherry sauce 120
    herring, apple and beetroot salad dressing 159
    marsala spice mix 223
    mint yoghurt sauce 52
    picada 43
    red wine-mustard sauce 245
    Thai beef salad dressing 139
    turkey gravy 197
Scandinavian baked ocean trout with apple and horseradish sauce 25
Seafood *see also* Fish
    kedgeree 143
    potted prawns 126

prawn and tomato curry 109
Semifreddo
 al torrone (nougat semifreddo) 161
 crunchy lime 162
Semolina gnocchi 160
Smoked salmon pancakes 207
Soufflé, twice baked cheese 178
Soup
 bollito misto 172
 buttermilk vichyssoise 213
 gazpacho 122
 green pea 213
 Lebanese cucumber 212
Spiced Christmas stars 210
Spiced peaches 209
Spinach, pea and sweet potato curry 223
Spring roast lamb with mint yoghurt sauce 52
Sticky date pudding 16
Stuffing
 Lombardy turkey 197
 roast chicken 41
 sausage, apple and cranberry 196
Sweet potato, pea and spinach curry 223
Tarte au citron 189
Tarts *see* Pies and pastries
Teabread, farmhouse 82
Terrines
 chicken, pork and veal with cherry sauce 120
 chicken liver 73
Thai beef salad 139
Thakkali 109
Tiramisu 246
Tomatoes
 gazpacho 122
 Panzanella 33
 pissaladiere 215
 prawn and tomato curry 109
 salmorejo 214
 salsa verde 173
Truffle terrine 67
Turkey
 Lombardy 197
 roasted with sausage, apple and cranberry stuffing 196
Twice baked cheese soufflé 178
Two-minute roast chicken stuffing 41
Veal
 pork and chicken terrine with cherry sauce 120
 pork fricadelles (meatballs) 136
Wholemeal banana bread 83

INDEX

Aga 12–13
Alice in Wonderland 95, 180–1, 183
Allen, Adrianne 51
Allen, Dave 90–1
America 49–51, 123–4
Amis, Martin 227
An Age of Kings 164–5, 167
Arthur, Jean 51
Ashcroft, Peggy 105
Austria 117–18
Ayckbourn, Alan 136–7, 212
Bacall, Lauren 135–6
Bangkok 137–8
Barford, Grace 37
"Barn Elms" 37, 80, 85–7, 165
Barrie, J.M. 233
Beat the Devil 113–14, 115, 125
Beerbohm, Sir Herbert 102–3
Bell, Vanessa and Clive 185–6
Bellow, Saul 227
Benjamin, Adrian 180, 181
Bennett, Alan 171
Bentine, Michael 185
Berenson, Bernard 186
Bergman, Ingrid 116, 166

Blackmore, Michael 56
Blanch, Leslie 119
Bloomsbury group 185–6
The Blue Bird 238
Bogarde, Dirk 53, 179
Bogart, Humphrey 113–14, 115
Boodle's Club 17–18, 31
Boxer, Arabella 18
Brinton, Ralph 94
Broadway 34, 48, 79
Brook, Peter 129–31
Brumas 49
Bryner, Yul 117–18
Buck's Club 17, 71–2, 74
Buck's Fizz 74
Buckmaster, Herbert "Buck" 34, 36–7, 39–40, 47–8, 70–2, 76–8, 238
Buckmaster, Joan see Morley, Joan
Buckmaster, John 30, 34, 36–7, 38–9, 74, 165
Budberg, Baroness Moura 190–1
Bull, Peter 34, 95, 97, 184
Burnham, Jeremy 90
Capote, Truman 113–14
Carrington, Dora 186, 187
The Chalk Garden 38, 85, 90
Chandler, Eileen 50
Chaplin, Charlie 50
Chappell, William 129
Chatto, Daniel 96
Chatto, Ros 166, 168, 170–2, 176–7, 180
Chatto, Tom 171, 177
Chez Peter 149–50
Christmas 10, 48, 50–1, 56–7, 90, 94, 100, 134, 169–70, 192–219
Churchill, Lady Clementine 188
Cleese, John 182
Colt House 7–8, 93, 146, 228
Conrad, Joseph 102
Cook, Mary 185, 188–9, 191, 222, 233

Cooper, Doris 40–1
Cooper, Gladys "G" 26, 30, 34, 36–41, 70, 71, 76–8, 85–7, 90, 97, 123, 165, 202, 233, 238
    America, in 47, 49–51, 53, 79–81
Cooper, Gracie 40, 87, 165, 239
Cooper, Tommy 185
Corbett, Ronnie 185
Counsell, Elizabeth 97
Counsell, John 97
Count Seruya "Foxy" 185
Coward, Noel 38, 79, 98
Crazies Hill 8, 36, 47, 48, 69, 94
Cromwell 121
Cukor, George 50
culture 132–3
Dare, Zena 51
Darwin 140–1
Dassin, Jules 119
Davis, Bette 86, 105
Dench, Judy 165
Denham Film Studios 35
Densham, Janet 149
Devonshire, Deborah 63
Dews, Peter 164
di Nobili, Lila 165
The Doctor's Dilema 148
Don, Margaret 164
Don's Party 142
du Maurier, Gerald 79
Duncan, Isadora 94
Dupleix, Jill 57
Durack, Terry 57
Edward My Son 48, 56, 123, 211
Edwards, Hilton 97
Edwards, Jimmy 154
Esbenson, Mogens Bay 139
Evans, Anne 164
Evans, Edith 90
Fairchild, William 108
"Fairmans" 5, 6, 7, 8–11, 29–32, 34–5, 37, 39, 61, 65, 90, 131, 133, 169–70, 171, 192, 230–1, 233–4, 237, 248
family holidays 125–6

Fanny 132–3, 134
Fass, Gertrude "Daisy" 18, 78
Fields, Gracie 51
Finch, Peter 156
Forbes, Meriel 104
Fox, Angela 177–8
Fox, Edward 177
Fox, Robert 177
Fox, Robin 110, 131, 177–8
Fox, William "James" 177, 178, 179–80
France 119–20, 170, 239
Frith, Nigel 181
Gabor, Zsa Zsa 116
Garbo, Greta 50
Garnet, David 186
Gaslight 184
Gate Theatre, Dublin 97
Gate Theatre, Notting Hill 34
Genghis Khan 166
Gilbert, Olive 51
Gilkes, Brian 12
Gilkes's Garage 11–12
godparents 95–7
Gow, Ronald 105
Gowing, Laurence 187
Gowing, Mrs see Strachey, Julia
Grant, Duncan 186
Gray, Charles 121–2
Guinness, Alec 121
Guthrie, Tyrone 248
gypsies 47, 69
Hall, Peter 165
Hampshire, Susan 171
Hancock, Tony 185
Hardwicke, Cedric 51
Hardy, Emma 39, 87, 220, 233
Hardy, Justine 39, 87, 233
Hardy, Robert "Tim" 39, 164–5, 167
Harris, Richard 121
Harrison, Rex 51, 165
Hart Davis, Comfort 150–1
Hauser, Frank 183
Havanna 74
Hawaii 123–4
Haycock, Mrs 12, 195

Hearn, Jaleh 88
Hearn, Peter 88
Hearst, Randolph 51
Henley 80, 81–2
Hicks, Seymour 79
Hill, Benny 185
Hiller, Wendy 105–7
Hillsden, Mrs 74
Hollywood 50, 53, 79, 116
Hotel Paradiso 119
housekeeping 9–11
How the Other Half Loves 88, 136–42, 212, 239
Howard, Arthur 154
Howard, Frankie 185
Howard, Irene 154
Howard, Leslie 105, 154
Howard, Ron 117
Howard, Trevor 103, 108
Hudson, Elaine 156
Hurst Lodge 96, 146, 153–7, 166–7
Huston, John 113–14
India 221–3, 226–7
Irving, Ellis 55
Italy 96, 113–17, 125–6, 161, 239–43
Jackson, Anne 117
Johnson, Celia 105
Jonas, John 11, 231
Jones, Bess 156
Jones, Jennifer 114, 115
The Journey 117
Kendall, Felicity 171
Kendall, Kay 79
Kerr, Deborah 117, 166
Korda, Alexander 102–4
La Fornace 241
Laughton, Charles 165
Leigh, Vivien 37–8
Leon, Ruth 64, 231, 234
A Likely Tale 134
Little, Charlie 88, 95, 142, 166, 221, 236, 241
Little, Daisy 96, 227
Little, Jack 96
The Little Hut 128, 129–31,

253

137, 171
Loder, Basil 51
Lollobrigida, Gina 114, 115
London 11, 38, 39, 41, 68, 71, 133, 147, 170–2
Longaretti, Tony 96, 161
Lonsdale, Freddie 51, 177
Losey, Joe 179, 190–1
Loukes, Nick 181
Love on the Dole 105
Love's Labour's Lost 183
Mabey, David 53
McGarry, Pat 74
MacLiammoir, Michael 97–8
McShane, Ian 123
Major Barbara 105
Majority of One 166
The Man who Came to Dinner 63
"Maplecroft" 89–90
Marie Antoinette 106
Matthew, Christopher 165
Maugham, Somerset 51, 79
Maugham, Syrie 51
Melbourne 48, 56–7, 140–2
Menuhin, Yehudi 192
Mercouri, Melina 119
Merivale, Daniel 37
Merivale, John "Jack" 37
Merivale, Philip 37, 78
Merivale, Rosamund 37, 38
Merivale, Valentine 37
Messell, Oliver 129
MGM Studios 50
Midgeley, Robin 141, 142
Miles, Christopher 178
Miles, Sarah 171, 178, 179–80
Mills, Juliet and Hayley 153
Milne, Noreen 155, 167
Minelli, Liza 50
Mitchum, Robert 102
Mitford, Nancy 119, 129–30, 192
Mitford sisters 63
Mond, Mary 36
Morley, Alexis 64
Morley, Annabel "Abbie" 44, 45, 46, 60, 69, 101, 111, 127,
128, 146
 acting 102–9, 110, 168, 181–4
 birth 47–8
 education 147–57, 164–7
 employment 180–1, 184–9, 190–1
 reading 176–7
 wedding 236, 239–40
Morley, Hugo 64
Morley, Joan (nee Buckmaster) 10–11, 22, 24, 26, 29–30, 36, 39, 43, 44, 46, 47–8, 59, 60, 70, 82, 87, 112, 115, 137, 145, 146, 150, 157, 193
 character 31, 98, 130–2, 171, 176, 230
 child, as 49, 74
 death 227–34
 marriage 28, 30–2, 34–5, 99
 Sydney, on 54–5
Morley, Juliet 64
Morley, Major Wilton 17–18, 31, 61
Morley, Margaret 36, 43
Morley, Robert 5, 6, 11, 12–13, 44, 46, 47–8, 59, 60, 69, 74, 100, 112, 128, 145, 146, 155, 191
 acting 11, 31, 34–5, 62, 86, 105–8, 131, 136–7, 148, 166, 211
 America, on 50–1
 background 30–1
 character 31–2, 43, 61, 64, 131–2, 177, 192–3, 238, 248
 chocolate 65
 death 227–8
 education, on 147–8
 films, 113–24, 156, 166, 238
 food, on 17, 32, 71, 88, 99, 149
 French, on the 120
 gambling 8, 18
 knighthood 22
 marriage 28, 30–2, 34–5
 Melbourne, on 57, 141
 plays 48, 90, 129–34, 136–45
 Sydney, on 55, 57, 142–3
 visitors, on 91–3
Morley, Sheridan "Sherry" 11, 29, 44, 45, 48, 50–1, 55–7, 59, 60, 63–5, 74, 87, 93, 105, 112, 113, 115–16, 127, 152–3, 181, 202, 228, 231–4, 237–8
Morley, Wilton "Will" 38, 39, 48, 60, 61–3, 64–5, 69, 71, 79–80, 89, 113, 117, 118, 125–6, 127, 135, 156, 230–4, 237
Moxon, Elizabeth 19
Murder at the Gallop 134
music 132–3, 154, 193
My Fair Lady 79, 93, 165
Neale, Gordon 241
Neville, John 156
New York 50–1
New Zealand 88–9, 160
Niven, David 50
Niven, Jamie 50
Niven, Primmie 50
Novello, Ivor 41, 51, 233
Now, Voyager 79
Old Nan 48–9, 59
Olivier, Laurence 37, 79, 104
Outcast of the Islands 102–9, 110
Oxford 181–4
Pacific Palisades 49–50, 79
Palmer, Lili 51
Parkinson, Michael 61
Partridge, Frances 186–8
Paton, Joe 85, 88
Pearsall Smith, Logan 186
Pearson, Margaret 62
Pearson, Neville 36, 77
Pearson, Nigel 37
Pearson, Sally 27, 36, 38, 39, 78, 87, 164–5, 229, 230, 233
Penny's Lane 9
Peter Pan 233
Phipps, Nick 34
Picon, Molly 166
Pinewood Studios 11
Playhouse Theatre 30, 74
Pleasted, Miss 12–13
Plowman, Mr and Mrs 9

254

Plowright, Joan 37
Prunier's 68
Pygmalion 105
Radziwell, Antony 180
Rating, John 97
Reading Technical College 152, 167, 169–70
Redgrave, Vanessa 79, 94, 165
Reed, Carol 102–3, 109
Rees, Angharad 171
Reiz, Karel 94
Relative Values 38
religious education 95–7
restaurant dining 17, 68, 72, 133, 149–50
Richard II 181, 183
Richards, Cyril 51
Richardson, Ralph 104–7, 111, 156
Ring Around the Moon 183
Robards, Jason 117
Roberts, Ivor 183
Robeson, Paul 165
Ross, Vivie 96
The Royal Hunt of the Sun 90
Rupert House 36, 149–52
Rutherford, Margaret 134
Saunders, George 116
Schell, Maximillian 119
Schilling, Barbara 181–2
Schofield, Paul 79, 171
seasonal food 10
Secombe, Harry 185
The Secret Garden 50, 79, 176, 186
Sellers, Peter 185
The Servant 179
Shaw, Tony 22
Shelmedine, Anne 164
Shepperton Studios 11, 106–7
Sheridan, Dinah 37
Silver, Mrs 12
Singh, Manjit 221
Sizewell Hall 152–3
Smith, Maggie 90, 166
Solve Your Problem (SYP) 185, 188, 190

The Song of Bernadette 79
Spain 121–2
Sri Lanka 103, 109
Stacey, Mrs 8, 12
staff 11, 12–13
Stainer, Doris 154
Stephens, Robert 90
Stewart, Sophie 55
Stokes, Sewell 11, 93–5, 97, 100, 106, 148, 156
Stott, Jonathan 90
Stott, Judith 90
Strachey, Julia 185–8
Strachey, Lytton 185, 186
Stratford 165
Stubbs, Nancy 48, 49, 106, 132, 150
Sweet Bird of Youth 135
Sydney 48, 54–6, 64, 211–12
Tagg, Alan 166
Tate, Nick 142
Taylor, Elizabeth 238
Taylor, Nellie 37
Tetzel, Joan 130, 137
Thailand 137–9
That Hamilton Woman 79
The Third Man 118
Thorneycroft, Lord and Lady 126
Tiger Bay 153
Tomlin, Stephen 186, 187
Tomlinson, David 131
Topkapi 119
The Trials of Oscar Wilde 156
Trocadero 133
Trollope, Joanna 13
Tuscany 96, 240–3
Tuyn, Harry 153
Ustinov, Peter 181
Ustinov, Tamara 181
Waiting for Godot 95
Wallace, Ian 133
Wallach, Eli 118
Wallis, Jenny 187
War and Remembrance 123
Wargrave 9, 11, 23, 35, 49, 69, 80, 97, 152, 176, 194

West, Rebecca 190
West End 48, 129, 166
Wilde, Oscar 34, 97, 156
Williamson, David 142
Wilson, Harold 22
Windsor, Duke and Duchess 126
Wynne Wilson, George 149

Acknowledgements

Thanks to Jane Curry and her team and especially to Sarah Plant for their enthusiasm, care and expertise.

Thanks to everyone who has eaten at my table and come back for more because cooks, like actors, need an appreciative audience.

Thanks to Charlie whose love, encouragement and support sustains me nearly forty years on from that first chocolate cake.